'TIL DEATH & BEYOND

THE HAUNTED JOURNEY OF JOHN AND STACEY EDWARDS

Based on the experiences and research of John and Stacey Edwards

Leprechaun Press
NEVADA

'TIL DEATH & BEYOND

THE HAUNTED JOURNEY OF JOHN AND STACEY EDWARDS

Based on the experiences and research
of John and Stacey Edwards

Copyright © 2019 Leprechaun Productions
All Rights Reserved.

No part of this publication may be reproduced or transmitted in any form or by any means, mechanical or electronic, including photocopying and recording, or by any information storage and retrieval system, without permission in writing from the author or publisher (except by a reviewer, who may quote brief passages in articles or reviews).

ISBN: 978-1-945950-11-7 (Paperback)

Published by:

Leprechaun Productions
Nevada

Cover design: Sam Shearon
www.mister-sam.com

Editor: A. Dale Triplett
@DaleTriplett

Book layout: SMAK
www.smakgraphics.com

Printed in the United States of America

'Til Death & Beyond   by John & Stacey Edwards

Table of Contents

	Foreword	p. 1
	Acknowledgements	p. 3
1	The Wrestler and The Witch	p. 7
2	The Event	p. 13
3	My Unidentified Flying Childhood	p. 17
4	The Money Spell and Other Miscues	p. 21
5	How Did You Not Hear That?	p. 27
6	They Hopped On Your Back	p. 33
7	The Madness of our Method	p. 41
8	A Field Of Theories	p. 49
9	The Keeper Theory	p. 57
10	Pay Per Boos	p. 63

11	THE THEORY OF FEAR	p. 69
12	ELECTRONIC SUMMONINGS	p. 75
13	THAT DARN CAT	p. 79
14	CHASING NEWPORT	p. 85
15	THE PHANTOM MENACE	p. 91
16	SPIRITS OF THE STAGE	p. 95
17	THE BLACK HOUSE	p. 101
18	THE PEOPLE AT THE DOOR	p. 109
19	THE HOUSE OF EDWARDS	p. 113
20	THE CONFEDERATE GHOST	p. 117
21	THE CURIOUS CASE OF MARY BATEMAN	p. 123
22	THE TRUCK STOP	p. 127
23	WHERE'S THE OTHER GUY?	p. 133
24	WE ARE ALL STRANGE HERE	p. 137
	ABOUT THE AUTHORS	p. 142

Foreword

Everyone has a great ghost story.

But most of society is willing to say, I don't believe in ghosts, BUT- then some say - I do think I've had an experience. Interesting....

Paranormal Investigation has practically become a national pastime; new teams of paranormal investigators seem to pop up every other day, however John and Stacey Edwards are by no means your every other day investigators.

It's one thing to watch a team doing their thing on TV, but seeing these two in action which I have - is a whole other can of scary...

John and Stacey are equipped with a wealth of knowledge and experience. They take you on a fascinating and "truth be told" journey into their OWN personal world of the Paranormal in this roller coaster ride of a read!

There are some amazing events in this book, of a wide variety of phenomena and each experience is quite intriguing. There's a lot to be learned here, between their fueled curiosity, Stacey's intense research and John's principled theories, they are able to reveal in every situation a direct relationship with history and their real life events.

Over the years, this couple has lived through some very curious unexplained circumstances, some more creepy than others. There's lots to be learned on this side of the veil.

Their chain of ups and downs that have taken place in their lives only leaves me wanting to know more. This is John and Stacey's real life experience with the supernatural.

Bonita Mann, Producer

'Til Death & Beyond by John & Stacey Edwards

Acknowledgements

A whole lot goes into writing a book.. but just like someone's first album, we believe your first book is your life's major inspiration to that point, while the follow up book is expected to somehow match that intensity with maybe a year's worth of stories? There was no way for us to include "everything" in this first book…in fact, we left out some major plot points entirely, for the simple fact they are, more than likely, their own story to themselves. What we did Include is a collection of some of the most amazing events from throughout our lives. A collection of events that actually start to gel together and make sense where none should ever be found. We also decided, because of the fact we cover most of our life, to include as many people who played a part in helping to have our story write itself and take shape. If we left you out…we probably meant to.

A huge thank you goes out to our wonderful daughters Rajja and Arianna! You both are the most giving, loving, and selfless ladies on the planet and always very supportive of your crazy parents! We love you more!!

To our son Dakota Edwards, who may very well be the creepiest one out of all of us! With the biggest heart to match. I love you "Kota" (Coty).

To Will, Josh, Nina, and "B"…hope you wouldn't actually think we'd forget about you and btw…we love you very much!

Kim, thank you for always believing in us, helping us out of hard spots, spreading the word about whatever crazy thing we're doing this week, and for always being the best big sister on this or any other planet.

A special dedication to "Mom" or Grandma Ruble who has ran our family like a BOSS for decades! She taught me how to treat people and how to freaking survive.

On the flip side of that, I miss you and love you very much Grandaddy. From all of the stories, I have taken after you my entire life!

Thank you to David Weatherly, who we knew was a kindred spirit from our first encounter…and on the subject of our favorite Paranormal Authors! Thank you to Nick Redfern, and Marie D. Jones for always helping to keep us informed and entertained as well!

Thank you Wes and Anita Forsythe for just being awesome! Wes, especially for inspiring me to be consistent!

To our soul sister Serena Gordon…you will always be our plus 1 !!!

Jef, I'm pretty sure you'll love this book. I'm going to leave you a copy bro. I still miss you.

Thank you to each and every single person who have spent their time joining us on The Paranormal Sideshow Podcast, The Haunted South Paranormal Podcast, or even The Third Side Podcast over the past decade!! We love all of you so much and are very thankful for people like Juan Cruz, Dr. Nico, Alan Turner, Bonnie, Jeff Carter, and so many more!! Truly, you keep us going!

Tim, Connie, and Ashleigh Clark who guided us through our darkest time and also gave us our platform to shine. There are no better people in this world than you guys!

To Frannie and the ETSU/JCCT Crew! From the Incredibly talented and beautiful daughters of Frannie to the old school crew of Joe, April, Kaeli, and Rachel!! God, we adore all of you so much!

Weston Leonard…man, we've banged heads, had fights, made each other mad, laughed, had amazing adventures, and truth be told…With No Wes there is No Haunted South Podcast, Paranormal Sideshow, And so much more. We both love you Wes and owe you much.

Bonita and Laura! Bo…hopefully you're reading this while sitting in a creepy location and telling us where to stand (wink wink) OMG! Our journey with you gals is only beginning yet already has helped us grow so much. Love you both!!!

Travis Moulden…our brother through so much. Your wisdom needs to be tapped into for a major book series at some point! For now, we'll keep using it for spiritual guidance bro.

ACKNOWLEDGEMENTS

Allen Marston…to watch you grow in the field has been an honor and a delight! As with Travis…you two hold a permanent seat at our "round table."

Bea…stay weird. Please.

My pro wrestling brothers of Chris Richards, Steve "Fury" Phillips, Tony Givens, Chase Owens, Mr. Bolo, Travis Leilich, Travis Dykes, Wayne Adkins, Bryan "Bubba" Wayne, Mikey Dugger, Doug Gibson, Codge Carter, and so many others!! You have all shared haunted locker rooms, scary road stories, and many unforgettable moments of my life.

Scotty Large…wow. I truly hope you come back as a ghost!

Travis Guinn, you have always and will always be my brother. I miss you and hate that we couldn't have stayed 10 years old forever. Aaron Smith, and Troy Owens…it's never too late to record that last album! I will always mark you guys as part of my inspiration.

Pat and Sandi.. thank you for so much fun, excitement, and knowledge. You both may never read this but still should know I felt your names deserve the spot.

Josh Hopkins, you deserve all the credit in helping me come out of the dark on things we experienced. I purposely stayed quiet until you and I experienced a night that changed our paradigm. Plus, we'll always have A.M.P.S.!!

To Mama and Daddy…I love you more than you'll ever realize. These events are also your story as you've experienced most of them as well!

Thank you to "In Search Of" for scaring the crap out of both of us as children!

To Stephen King for starting Stacey's journey into the wasteland many moons ago!

To Sir Arthur Conan Doyle for being John's reason for always trying to find a mystery (whether there is one or not).

Kyler, know how special you are! Your magic is just beginning.

The Wrestler & the Witch

The Wrestler and The Witch

The smell of my parents' floral print couch was something I was all too familiar with. Sometimes it offered a bit of safety and security to me when struggling with a hard day. This morning was a tougher decision than most as I had met a girl last night…a girl who was amazing to be around…and I had stayed at her place the entire night.

I was coming off a tremendously bad relationship that had put my life into a definite tailspin. I kept telling myself "this is the last thing you need, you're only 21 years old," but it felt exactly the opposite. She had given me a piece of paper with her phone number scribbled on it. So there I lay on that uncomfortable couch facing the back.

My mom, who was very sick and in bed, was sleeping in the back of the house, leaving me as the only other person home on this beautiful Saturday morning in May of 1997. I was gripping that piece of paper while running the previous night through my overactive mind. I was becoming restless with my indecisiveness and flipped over to face the picture window of the living room.

As I was laying there contemplating my next move, I closed my eyes only to hear my mom talking to me. I opened my eyes without moving my body and stared up at my mother standing across the room in front of my dad's recliner. I didn't yet notice the differences in her from what I knew to be the truth.

Mom started telling me many things and, in fact, she was fussing at me. I can't give a word by word account of this because I have tried so hard to forget the encounter. What I can tell you is she was trying her best to keep me from calling the girl back. She was making her case as to all of the reasons it should never have happened and absolutely why it shouldn't go any further.

I remember answering my mom rather angrily, and right about

that time I heard a voice come from the back of the house. The voice was very familiar and soothing to my soul, as it was the voice of my actual mother. It was at this time I felt like a veil had been lifted off of my eyes! I stared at this woman in my parents' living room who had been trying to prevent me from calling the sweet girl I'd stayed the night with.

The woman before me was indeed a vision of my mother, except it was my mom as she had been in her early twenties, before she had ever become sick with an autoimmune disorder, one that basically forced her into bed daily. It was my mom before she had weight gain, hair loss, and a declining quality of life that rips at my heart from knowing the strong and beautiful lady she was before Lupus.

The false vision of my mother just stood there staring at me without vanishing! I could hear my mom hollering from the bedroom to ask if it was me she heard. "John, John honey, are you talking to someone?" Going back to this moment still gives me chills over my entire body. I pulled every ounce of courage inside of myself and answered her "yeah, mom, it's me, but I'm alone."

When I forced myself to speak to my real mother the imposter disappeared. I sat there in total astonishment trying to figure out what in the actual hell had just happened to me. I felt then as I feel now…I needed this girl in my life. I needed the name written above the phone number. I needed to call this girl that caused some unknown force to try and fool me into not calling. I needed Stacey.

I can honestly admit I wouldn't be here today if not for my "lovely wife", as Stacey has affectionately been named at the beginning of every single episode of our podcast. When I met her it was something straight out of a cheesy 90's drama movie. I was lost in a dark and depressing fog at that point in time, and Stacey was somewhere stuck inside of that same foggy dream.

Even though I was only 21 years old, I had seen way too much for someone my age. I had been in trouble more times than not, lived in several states already, and had given up on anything that had to do with love after a string of poor choices.

Stacey had also already seen like 40 years worth of B.S. and pain all nicely tucked away in her own 22 years. She had a near death experience a year before I met her, some very rough relationships, a strict upbringing, and a true love of the paranormal and metaphysical.

We both happened to be at our favorite location at the same time. It was Friday May 2nd, 1997 and we were two young, broken, and lonely kids trying to drink away some problems in a small bar known as "The Shore" in Bristol, Tennessee.

Stacey was attending college and I had already been a General Manager of a large retail chain by that point. We were from very different worlds and had no idea of just what kindred spirits we actually were.

I was standing at the bar and gripping my Bud Light tightly looking around for my friends. There was a band playing current covers and the little bar that normally hosted my friend's metal bands was pretty busy that night with a different crowd, the ones that only came for this band…and for the dreaded techno night. I usually avoided the nights like this one.

As I looked around someone captured my attention. There she was…the very vision of my boyhood dreams. A girl that looked the way I would draw if someone asked what I liked in a girl. Long black hair, skinny, yet with great hindquarters, and a mysterious look to her eyes. Oh my God her eyes…a million stories seem to always be hiding behind those eyes (and still do…considering the witches' mark and all). She was looking at me and I was looking at her. We danced, we kissed, we just became one in a matter of minutes. I knew she was everything I needed in my life. The rest, as they say, would be history, except for this one fact: we had no idea that during this innocent, young, romantic night of love, it would be the beginning of a journey neither of us could have ever expected.

Many strange and wonderful things occurred to us that first year. A couple of those things have defined our entire life together. From the morning after encounter with something pretending to be my mom, to the "event" that changed the actual course of both of our lives.

Some things about our story will just simply have to wait until a later date. Some things we will possibly hint to or tell a story that associates with that part of our life. You see, we felt it to be a bit pretentious to write an autobiography at this point. Instead, we want to share the things so fantastic and surreal that even we have a hard time comprehending them.

Stacey has magic in her veins. If she asks the universe for

something and lights a few candles, it always seems to work. Me? I was a lifelong opponent of the metaphysical until…well, until I could no longer ignore it. All of this we will be making far more clear to you later in the book.

I can say this much, I could write several books about my years as a professional wrestler. All of my road trips, my hundreds of episodes of local tv, and my role as the frontman lead singer of my band I named "Deadlevel" (for obvious reasons).

Deadlevel

In professional wrestling, I was the top "heel" or bad guy in the local area for well over a decade. If I was on the poster with my group of fellow rule breakers (J.H.P. Or John Hawkins Promotions, as my working name was John Hawkins), it was a guaranteed full house of fans to witness me, Steve Fury, and Chris Richards leave a trail of broken bones and broken egos in our path.

Wrestling was an early love and dream of mine, but my favorite part of it was the show aspect. I could control that crowd with a simple expression on my face. As I mentioned before, the stories from these days probably deserve their own book due to the unbelievable bond we all shared.

THE WRESTLER AND THE WITCH

My other dream as a kid was to perform my original songs in front of people. Deadlevel gave me the opportunity to record two independently financed albums and perform many local shows over the course of five years.

Behind the performer I was always a businessman. I have held business management jobs since I was in my late teens. I worked my way up over the years to managing entire districts of stores for a Fortune 500 retail company.

But at the core of all of those things was Stacey. She pushed me to follow all of my dreams. To sing my songs, become a wrestler, be an executive—to be everything people told me I couldn't be. She is my muse and my reason for doing anything I've ever done.

At the core of all of this was the one thing - and the only thing - we shared aside from our love of each other and our family. An event that forever changed and guided our path in this world.

You see, through everything we've ever done, we could be found in some run down old house, in a graveyard, or in a dusty old occult shop on the nights I wasn't chasing a dream. We were always chasing our destiny and chasing the answers to the big question. Why us? Why did it happen to us?

We've been chasing these answers for twenty years now. A large and colorful cast of characters have come and gone from our world during this time. The void that remains is the need to find answers for ourselves and for others who face the same paradigm shifting events that we did. People have come and gone, dreams have been fulfilled, and yet we are still searching all because of one day, one moment, and one event.

Stacey has magic in her veins

'Til Death & Beyond by John & Stacey Edwards

The Event

After the night John and I met, we were inseparable, only spending time apart when he had to be at work and I had to be at school. I was taking a few courses during the summer, including a writing class in which I had to do a lengthy research paper. The topic I chose for the paper was past life regression, a topic I still find fascinating. At the time I was obsessed with learning everything about magic, religions, spirits, and life after death. One of the things John and I loved about each other was the ability to just sit and talk for hours about these subjects. We both grew up in strictly religious households, where paranormal subjects were basically taboo.

One afternoon, we went to a little hole-in-the-wall, New Age shop to look for books. I was looking for more information on past life regression and John was looking for trouble. He picked up a book called *Invoking The Spirit* and decided to get it. Later that evening, we decided to take out the Ouija board, light some candles, and play around trying to contact spirits. I know, I know, it was stupid, but we made the mistake of thinking it was just a game. John took out his newly acquired book and flipped to the very end to find the spell to invoke a spirit. I strongly suggested that perhaps he should read the entire book before trying the spell, but, as I now know after years of marriage, John never reads the directions. After gathering a mirror, more candles, and the other items on the list and setting them up according to the diagram in the book, he was ready. Of course I willingly went along with the whole thing.

For anyone that knows John personally, or listens to our podcast, you know that he has a power all his own. It's in his voice and the commanding way he can turn a phrase (or a spell) into art. He drew on this power, and with a booming voice he recited the chant word for word. When he was finished, a very strange feeling overtook us both, the candles danced, and the mood darkened. We had no idea what these feelings and energies meant, and since we didn't see a ghost appear anywhere, we assumed it didn't work.

The next day, after seemingly forgetting about our drunken night of ritual magic, we were settling in for a night at home with some good food and drinks. John was in the kitchen cooking hamburgers and I was on the couch in the living room watching Wheel of Fortune. The duplex I lived in was small and had no air conditioning. Being July, it was very hot, so we had the front door, the back door, and all the windows open.

The kitchen was at the back of the house, and John was near the back door. A wall separated the kitchen from the living room. The couch was against the wall in the living room and the television was across the room against the other wall. There was a window to my right, at the end of the couch. This window had a very cheap shade covering it. You know, one of those shades you get from the Dollar store and as soon as you pull it down too far just once, it breaks and won't roll back up until you hand roll it from the top. We could not see each other, but what happened next changed us both forever.

John saw it first.

"As I was cooking, I felt a need to look to my right, like some 6th sense that allows you to feel danger or know someone is standing behind you. I looked over and saw a black, solid, shadow of a man running into the screen door from the outside and through the kitchen! This shadow man was approximately 6 feet tall with both legs, both arms, and honestly was more intense, as it was in a well lit room of ambient lighting. The "shadow" ran from the kitchen and into the room where Stacey was watching Pat Sajak tell corny jokes on national television.

The next thing I heard was the window shade, which was broken, actually roll up at a super speed! I knew what the sound was without even seeing it happen. Stacey then yelled to me from the living room saying "John..." and I replied "I don't want to talk about it"...and we didn't, for probably a week."

As I was sitting on the couch trying to figure out the latest puzzle (I love puzzles), I saw something out of the corner of my eye from the kitchen door. It ran between me and the television. I had been staring at the tv so intently that I clearly saw what moved in between. It was a "man," a completely black shadow figure, that was so dark it blocked out the television completely. I could make out his head, body, arms, and legs. It appeared in a running position.

The shadow ran straight out the window beside me. When it hit the window, the shade made a loud noise and rolled up very quickly. I sat stunned, just staring at the window for what seemed like a very long time. My mind was racing, spinning out of control, and I could feel it crashing. I then did what I always do in scary or confusing situations, I yelled for John. He didn't want to talk about it and I was fine with that. We eventually did sit down and talk about it a week later. It took that long to really get our heads together, and when we did, we were different.

This event shaped what is "John and Stacey Edwards" from that moment on. We have been each other's rock for 20 years of love, research, mysteries, learning, and most importantly, laughing at just how insane the story of our life together truly is.

After the "event" we were different

'Til Death & Beyond by John & Stacey Edwards

My Unidentified Flying Childhood

My mom is as sound as they come. She has been with one man her entire life, my Pop, whom she married at 18, and she is also as Christian as they come. She has been horrified by my pursuits for more than 20 years, but understands them at the same time. She is very sick and in terrible health due to first having Lupus along with many other but less severe problems. The doctors have made no bones about the fact she doesn't have very long left with me.

I have always had strange memories since early childhood—seeing shadows outside my window, having the entire family outside looking at lights over the mountain, and many nights of fear. I remember my mom being hysterical at times and the family calming her down, talking about something to do with UFOs but that's all I remember from my youngest days.

You might be saying "Hold your horse a second, John - I thought this was a book about ghosts and ghost hunting?" Well, a lot of individuals relate the word paranormal to only dealing with hauntings and ghosts. However, the paranormal also include those themes regarded to be outside the range of parapsychology; including clairvoyance, telepathy, faith healing, ESP, cryptozoology, UFOs and many other subjects. The world of the unknown is rife with things that go bump in the night, and we'd all be remiss if we didn't expand our horizons and thinking to include the broader realm of all those things that have yet to be explained.

When I'd grown a few years I had a first cousin in the military stationed out west near Las Vegas. I distinctly recall him bringing my family documents he had supposedly stolen. I remember being at a family reunion when he was showing everything to a close family member. Like I said, I was young but overheard him talking about UFO's and he said he was working there. This would have been around

85-87, I think. I remembered him going AWOL and being on the run. We had to take him money and food to various motels. I do know he went back because he was out of the service with a civilian job not long after that.

Haunted South

After a year or so of doing the Haunted South Paranormal Podcast, my cousin contacted me via Facebook for the first time in 15 years. He told me he loved my show and my interests in UFOs, saying"…We need to meet, I have some truly amazing things to share with you…I can't say it on here!" A few days later his Facebook page was deleted (I still have the messages from the disabled account) and I've not heard from him again. I would like to think I could find him but to no avail… strange, huh?

After another episode of the podcast, my mother called me into her room and told me to close the door, saying she had something serious to discuss with me. She told me she would only talk about this once, but because of what I was doing she felt it was important that I knew the truth. She wanted to explain why I had a weird memory from childhood of an angel taking me into the sky. I recalled playing outside on my swing set when I was maybe three years old, and Mom was in the house with the windows open, sometime during the summer in the 1970's, and I could hear her talking to her friends. Something started lifting me in the air but I wasn't scared at all. I saw my house and swing getting smaller and smaller as a comforting voice told me things…I honestly can't remember anything it said other than "don't worry, you're going to be ok," and that I had a purpose or mission.

Mom proceeded to tell me point blank when I closed the door that we had a UFO encounter. She said we were both outside playing on a nice summer afternoon around midday. Our house was on top of a hill in a neighborhood where there should or could have been witnesses, but there are none that I know of. She said it looked like a saucer from an old 1950's sci fi movie and wasn't very big at all. It was silver and silent just coming down over us. She picked me up in her arms to run inside and says I pointed up to it…She looked up and there was a blinding light. She told me she remembered things being done to her but that she didn't want to release my hand. She wouldn't go into any detail from on board, but did describe what we know to be the grays.

The next thing she knew we were both awake in her bed and silent. I was holding her hand very tightly but not saying a word and several hours had passed. She immediately phoned my dad at his work but he made fun of her so bad that she hushed it forever.

She doesn't want any fame or recognition for the event but simply wanted me to know that she believed it to be the reason for my encounters and for her sickness. She, like me, has been haunted her entire life.

Since then, I've had more experiences that are absolutely beyond explanation. Including being found outside asleep on the ground on more than one occasion. One of these times was in 2002 or so when Stacey found me outside and naked on our front porch.

After finding me I had a red mark on the back of my arm. I still carry this mark to this day, and it can only be described as what is known as a "scoop mark" in UFO circles. We still never know what the night is going to hold in store for us once we lay down for bed.

I also deal with a great deal of daily body pain that numerous doctors have zero explanation for. After blood test after blood test, nothing can ever pinpoint my issues. Otherwise, I'm a picture of perfect health.

I don't claim to be a victim of alien abduction on a calling card. I don't even really want it to be any part of what defines me, but what I do want is answers. I believe my mom, I trust my memories, and I can't explain the strangeness of my Unidentified Flying Childhood.

'TIL DEATH & BEYOND BY JOHN & STACEY EDWARDS

THE MONEY SPELL AND OTHER MISCUES

When John and I started investigating the paranormal, it was not easy to get a lot of quality information. We lived in the heart of the bible belt. People didn't talk about ghosts and other "works of the devil." Going to the bookstore was just as bad. In the largest bookstore in the area, there was maybe one shelf of books in the "New Age" section and looking there would garner you some strange sideways glances from the folks perusing the large section of Bibles and Christian literature right beside it. There was the one New Age shop in a little hole in the wall building in the area, you know, the place where John bought the book that most likely started our journey. But it went out of business shortly thereafter.

Needless to say, we made a few blunders. Ok, more than a few. And they weren't all mistakes that had to do with paranormal investigations. One of our biggest flubs was something we did to ourselves. It started with that first night and the spell to invoke a spirit. You would think that since our first attempt at "spellwork" went so incredibly wrong, we would be more careful with what we played around with. This was not the case. The truth is, the first spell worked, just not how we expected. For some reason, this made us think we should try something else, something that would help us. A money spell. At the time, money was really tight, we had some bills we needed to take care of, and this was our solution. We researched, gathered ingredients, performed the ritual, and buried the charm in the yard. We were absolutely sure it would work exactly the way we planned, with no ill side effects. Boy, were we wrong.

Now, I'm not saying the spell didn't work. It did, but in doing it we made a horrible mistake. Instead of just doing the spell for what we needed, we were greedy and asked for much more. In the months that followed, three very distinct things happened. Two of my relatives passed away, each leaving me a sum of money. Then, John got hurt at work. He had to have several operations on his elbow, and the company settled a large worker's comp claim with him. So, we did get money, just like we wanted, but we lost two family members and John's elbow in the process.

It turns out, I learned a very important lesson. Everything has a price. If you are greedy and try to take what you are not entitled to, you will pay for it in some way. In the time since then, I also learned if you do good things, give to others, and have a positive attitude, good things will happen to you and for you. Karma is real.

Everything has a price

Back to investigating the paranormal. In the beginning, we mostly relied on other people we met, we watched every documentary and television show we could, and learned by trial and error. A lot of our "lessons" we learned were from mistakes we made while investigating. For example:

Lesson #1: Know with whom you are investigating.

One thing we learned pretty quickly was to make sure you KNOW YOUR TEAM! Know everything about them, what their voice sounds like on recordings, whether or not their stomach constantly makes noise, if they fidget when they are supposed to be still, and what weird noises they make when they think they are being quiet. Funny enough, I used to hum when it was very quiet. I didn't even know I was doing it. John asked me about it once and I had no idea what he was talking about. He actually had to play a recording of me so I could hear it. After that, I caught myself doing it without even thinking. It was a surprisingly hard habit to break. It is important to know if anyone makes these weird sounds, otherwise your audio evidence will be compromised. Even the tiniest belly growl can sound like a demon from hell on a digital recorder.

Along with getting to know everyone's quirks, make sure you know enough about the members of your team to know their integrity is on a level with your own. If just one person puts out bad evidence, or fakes something, the whole team will suffer for it.

Lesson #2: There is such a thing as too many people.

One mistake we made early on was having a team that was too large. Too many people just spoil an investigation, even in very large locations. It makes it impossible to know every person and their unique characteristics. Eventually, we scaled down and made a much smaller team of people we knew well and trusted. If there were other people that wanted to investigate with us or bring a friend to "try it out," we just held a public event at a location we knew was active.

Lesson #3: Provocation should only be used under specific circumstances and not as a regular technique.

Provoking spirits is when you go into a location and yell, curse, say mean and hateful things, and challenge the spirits in hopes of garnering a response. While this does tend to work, there is one major problem. When you put that much negative energy into a location, what you get back will almost always be negative. Negative spirits are drawn to negative energy and emotions, especially anger. There are some situations where you may want to use provocation, but you better know what you are possibly getting yourself into.

Lesson #4: Be of sound mind.

Do not investigate if you are not emotionally sound. If you are depressed, anxious, over-stressed, or have some type of mental illness that is not being treated, you should think twice about going on an investigation. If you just broke up with your boyfriend or girlfriend, got fired from your job, have problems with family, whatever it is, wait until you feel better before dealing with spirits. Any type of emotional stress makes you vulnerable to spirit attachment, especially from the negative kind that want to oppress you.

Being emotionally compromised is a weakness that can be taken advantage of. It is impossible to know what you will encounter at a location, so even if you think it will be fine, and you swear a good investigation will make you feel better, it's unwise to chance it.

Lesson #5: Close your sessions and don't take anything home with you.

After a few nasty house guests, we finally learned that when an investigation is over, declare the sessions to be closed, and state that no spirits can follow you home. I can't tell you how many times we brought something home with us in the beginning, and didn't really realize why it was happening. We were opening lines of communication with the other side, opening doors, and then just leaving. Looking back now it seems obvious, but at the time, we just didn't think about it. For days after an investigation we would see black shapes out of the corner of our eyes or hear strange noises we had never heard before.

Lesson #6: Protect yourself.

This sounds like it should have been an easy and obvious lesson, but John and I didn't do this at first. We absolutely believed in ghosts, after all, we saw one with our own eyes! But we didn't do any type of protection against negative spirits, not at first anyway. It wasn't until some bad things started happening to us and our family in our own home that we took the protection seriously. Don't ever think that bad things can't happen to you. They *can* and they *will* if you are not careful. Wear crystals, say a prayer, use sage, carry a protection amulet, whatever feels right to you. Better safe than sorry.

It's strange to think back to the beginning and how different we were then. Mistakes will still be made, but, even after all this time, we are still learning and still moving forward.

'Til Death & Beyond by John & Stacey Edwards

How Did You Not Hear That?

Living with someone who has a psychic gift is a truly amazing experience. Watching John use his gift to help other people or to help spirits makes me love him more and more. Granted, there was an adjustment period at first. I realized pretty quickly that if I am upset, bored, or hungry, John knows without me telling him. Sometimes our family movie nights are interrupted by a spirit that just needs some help or has a message to deliver. Even going to places where people are very emotional, like hospitals and funeral homes is difficult. I find it particularly interesting that John, who was strictly against psychics, should develop this particular talent. He used to make it a point to not rely on anyone who claimed to be psychic, even going so far as to fire an entire team of investigators that claimed to have abilities.

John is not one of those people who had the gift his entire life. Instead, it sort of came on gradually. At first, we weren't even really sure what was happening. We started noticing it on investigations, during EVP (Electronic Voice Phenomenon) sessions. As the questions were being asked, John would claim he heard responses. He would tell us "someone said yes" or "I heard the name Billy." My first response was always, "Really?", to which he would respond, "Yes, really!" Of course, no one else heard anything. After the session was over, we would play the recording back to check for EVPs. Almost every time John said what he heard, there was an EVP of exactly what he said, right there on the recording.

Now, as amazing as this was, it was also incredibly frustrating. We did not know at the time that John could actually hear spirits, so we thought he was hearing disembodied voices the rest of us were just missing. We were all put out that we weren't experiencing these amazing voices that were obviously there, and John constantly had a high level of annoyance at the rest of us for not paying close enough attention. Pretty soon, the most common phrase at the investigation was "How did you not hear that?" Honestly, we had no idea.

John has had the gift his entire life

Eventually, it became clear what was happening. At first, John had no control over what he heard or when, but over the years he has been able to not only learn how to manage his gift, but also to improve it and make it stronger. We even use it on investigations now as a tool. John is still adamant that we do not use the gift as proof of a haunting. Instead, he uses his ability to direct the investigation to the areas that he feels the activity is strongest, or where he suspects a spirit is hanging out.

One of the most amazing parts of his gift is his ability to really get activity to happen around him. One of the running jokes with our old team was to say, "If you want something paranormal to happen, go with John." This is still true. The spirits just seem to flock to him and are always interested in what he is doing. This is one of the major contributing factors to our belief that so called "residual hauntings" are either very rare or nonexistent.

A residual haunting is the idea that a spirit is just going through the motions of their previous life, over and over, like a tape recorder, with no knowledge of the people around them. We have personally never come across a spirit that we were not able to interact with in some way. Even a spirit that appears to do the same things over and over can be pulled from their routine. I am not saying there are not residual hauntings, just that they are not as common as we once thought. We mostly get intelligent activity.

Perhaps it's not a matter of whether or not a spirit can communicate, but instead it depends on the ability of the person trying to initiate the communication. Some people just get more activity than others, like John. A great example of this is an EVP we captured during a public investigation at the Major Graham Mansion.

We were taking a tour of about ten people through the mansion and explaining some of the activity we found during our many investigations. We went to the basement, a true hotbed of activity, and decided to do a Frank's Box session for the group. The Frank's Box uses radio frequency sweeping technology. Basically, it is a device that sweeps through every radio station very quickly, producing white noise and giving the spirits an opportunity to use various frequencies to communicate.

John turned on the Frank's Box and started explaining what it was and how it worked. I was recording the session on my digital recorder. One thing I have noticed over the years is that sometimes spirits don't like to talk through the box, but they will use the energy of the white noise and produce some amazing EVPs.

Anyway, John was talking about how the sweep technology works, and how sometimes we would pick up long sentences that spanned several stations. He mentioned that, on several occasions, we even heard curse words come through the box that would not be heard on the actual radio stations. At this time, on my recording, there is a very clear EVP of a spirit saying, "He said we curse!" This still makes me giggle, as I can just imagine a couple of spirits standing with the crowd for John's presentation and being appalled that he suggested they should use such foul language. This is not the only instance of getting EVPs around what John was doing. I have recorded during the setup phase of our investigation and gotten EVPs from a spirit commenting on the position of our cameras, or how the DVR screen looks.

There are times when John suggests I spend some time alone in a particular location because he knows I will get some activity. While filming our documentary at the Major Graham Mansion, John decided I needed to be alone in the closet in a particularly active room of the house. A small, dark, creepy closet! I took a camcorder in with me, and a high gain microphone to allow those not locked up in the creepy closet to hear any EVPs in real time. It was completely pitch black in there, so I turned the camera on night shot and pointed it at my face, "Blair Witch" style.

I started by announcing that I wanted to communicate with any spirits that were in the closet. Then I asked, "Is anyone in here with me?" I did not hear anything at the time, but the others did. John told me what he heard, but I feel like he downplayed it a bit to keep me from freaking out. When you listen to the audio on the camera you can hear me ask if anyone is in the closet with me, and then there is a very deep, scratchy voice that says, "I'm in here with you."

John can even garner activity in places that you would think had no activity. Another joke our team used to make was, "John can go out into the middle of a field and *still* get EVPs!" Funny enough, we tried that as well, and got one of the best EVPs we have ever captured. It happened in Johnson City, Tennessee at the site of the recently demolished Swingle Hospital.

Every town has their alleged "haunted locations" where rumor and legend prevail over truth, and scary stories are told at campfires and slumber parties. Swingle was no exception, with tales of a mad doctor who butchered his patients, mass graves on the grounds, and ghostly sightings of former victims haunting the building. None of this is true, of course, but the stories live on regardless.

The Swingle Hospital was opened in early 1948 by three doctors. The president of the hospital, Hugh Swingle, had trouble keeping doctors in residence, as they would often move on to pursue further education and opportunities. As a result, Swingle closed the practice in the 1960's and the building stood vacant for decades. This building was actually a very large, beautiful house. Over the years of being abandoned, the house fell into disrepair. Even run down and boarded up, it was by far the most beautiful house in the city, one of my favorites. Unfortunately, kids would break in and vandalize the property, hoping to catch sight of a ghost, or just to brag to their friends that they spent the night there. The house was unsafe, and since the family couldn't keep people away from it, they made the decision in 2010 to have it torn down.

It just so happens that we know someone who knows someone, and we were able to get permission to investigate the plot of land where the hospital once stood. We wanted to see if we could still get activity associated with the hospital, even though it was gone. We were, quite literally, in the middle of a field. John was asking the questions, and they were mostly aimed at any spirits that were still around from the hospital. He asked, "Is there anything we can do for you?" Although we heard nothing at the time, when John reviewed the recording, a spirit very clearly says, "We're not in need of helping." I still get chills when I hear it.

Over the past few years, John and I have worked on finding ways to use his gift to help stir up the activity even more on our investigations. I have stopped questioning if he really heard something, and he has stopped asking me if I heard what he heard. Instead, I just tell him if I hear something. It saves a lot of time that way.

'Til Death & Beyond by John & Stacey Edwards

They Hopped On Your Back

The danger of living with the paranormal is a very real thing. We have all read the firsthand accounts of those unfortunate people who were targeted by some unseen force from the other side of the veil. These hauntings can go on for days, weeks, months, or in very severe cases, it can last for years.

What causes a ghost or inhuman entity to become attached to a piece of land, a home, or even a human being? We have potential theories of dead lovers, unfinished business with a family member, a house they loved or built, or even an object they cherished in life. The truth of the matter is nobody is entirely sure as to why this occurs with some people, and with others you don't hear a peep, even from someone you may actually hope to hear from again.

Regardless of the reason, many times when we have been called in to investigate a home or a business, it's because something is attached to a particular person in that place. As with everything in this field, let me add "not always is this the case," as "absolutes" are few and far between in this rodeo.

Something we have become all too familiar with over the years is the other way an attachment begins. This is sometimes from being careless, and sometimes it's simply because someone takes a liking or a disliking to you. I also feel that, on rare occasions, it's because you are their ticket out of a building they couldn't leave on their own. And these attachments are the ones associated with being part of a paranormal investigation.

When I started investigating the paranormal, there wasn't a wealth of Ghost Hunting 101 books available for the studious ghost hunting apprentice. Sure, you had Hans Holzer, the Warrens, various local books, and a small amount of documentaries. Yet I don't remember many of those mentioning the real dangers associated with paranormal investigating.

I am positive that Stacey and I accidentally attached an evil spirit to us in '97, that we had astral critters with us for awhile, and that I took many other various ghosts home with me from investigations for many years. I always refused to do any cleansings or blessings before or after an investigation, because I was worried about messing up my evidence gathering ability. I wasn't always aware as to why I captured so much more evidence than my fellow investigators. This practice seemingly made me a paranormal "über" for many a restless spirit in my early days of investigating.

By the time 2006 arrived, I was finally opening myself up to taking precautions before and after investigations due to the birth of our baby girl. The last thing I would ever want to do would be to put sweet Arianna in any kind danger due to daddy's stupidity.

For a couple of years we were dealing with more than enough from the Black House—a tale you'll read about soon—without needing to add fuel to that dumpster fire. I was becoming pretty cautious, yet I was still being targeted over other investigators. I was always the one people went with if they wanted to experience something insane. (We understand all of that much more these days.)

By 2010, this was old hat for me, and I was fairly confident nothing could really surprise me anymore. I believe that line of thinking in the paranormal field is perhaps the most careless of all. There will always be something to come along that is brand new and unexplainable.

We had just moved from the Black House and were honestly trying to repair ourselves. In hindsight, you would think this would be a great time for me and Stacey to focus on that photography hobby we always wanted to pursue, right? Nope, not us, because we found this to be an almost spiritual (no pun intended) experience hunting ghosts together. Nothing brings us closer than doing this together. In fact, we make many other couples question the health of their own relationships after hanging out with the two of us.

So, there we were, investigating a three story former bank building in Kingsport, Tennessee. This building was legitimate as far as hauntings are concerned. Every floor, including the basement, had its own unique haunting. The basement was something dark and powerful. The first

They Hopped On Your Back

floor was just heavy feeling. The third floor had a more playful spirit that liked to mess with our gear. But the second floor had some of the strangest.

While investigating the second floor, we (my longtime partner in crime Tim Clark, Stacey, and I) were basically doing some simple "call and response" when I suddenly felt this electrified type feeling I refer to as being "charged." It's never a good thing to feel.

Upon reviewing the evidence from this area, we captured a piece of evidence that truly shook us to the core. It reaffirmed to us the fact that you have no business investigating when you are emotionally weakened, as we both were at this point in time.

Audio review

The EVP we captured simply replied to me talking about feeling heavy and charged all of a sudden. A voice replied *"They Hopped On Your Back"* and I knew instantly what that meant. As I was weak, not taking precautions, and had no guard up whatsoever, I was prime real estate for an escaping spirit to take for a joy ride. It took me a few visits to this place to shake that one.

My greatest attachment, though, is an ongoing story in my life. It's a story I will discuss without divulging every aspect, just yet. I will, however, tell you that I picked up an attachment in 2010 at a location known as the Major Graham Mansion in Max Meadows, Virginia. The attachment is a female associated with the history of the property, and she has become known to a few others along the way.

During one of the Scarefest events in Lexington, Kentucky that Stacey and I attended, I had one of the most eye opening experiences of my life. The entire weekend I experienced a terrible headache that I just couldn't shake. I had many "psychics" come up to our table where we were giving away free copies of one of our documentaries. They would all basically say the same thing, "I'll bet it's difficult for you being in here around all these people." It was just bizarre man. I'm a talker and a people person, if I'm anything at all.

The weirdness continued throughout all three days. We were beside the booth of this adorable little Southern Belle medium named Serena Gordon, and boy oh boy does she end up playing a significant part in our story from that point forward.

Anyways, after three days, Serena was always pretty calm doing her readings, using tarot cards to get her vibes going as she would see client after client. I kept feeling weird and Stacey kept nagging me to get a reading. Finally, it was Sunday afternoon and we were starting to pack up when Stacey went and asked Serena if she could give me a reading. I reluctantly accepted the command and assumed my position across from the medium.

The reading began and instantly the crap hit the fan! Serena started describing Major Graham Mansion and we, up to that point, had told NOBODY about our first visit to the property! It hadn't been on any tv shows and there was really no way for her to know what she knew.

The intensely haunted Major Graham Mansion

She went on to talk about how I had picked up an attachment there. She told me this attachment enjoyed grabbing spirits and bringing them back to me because of how excited I would get. Then the power of this attachment became too much and Serena lost her cool! Needless to say, I probably required a change of my underoos after this reading.

Serena was able to give us another piece of information that day that didn't happen for six years! But, when it did happen, it happened exactly the way she said it would. Like I said before, there is a huge piece of this story that will absolutely be told…when the time is right.

As far as the attachments go, the things we have experienced are countless and have helped shape the way we prepare for investigations. The dangers of the paranormal are all too real for even the seasoned investigator. When you least expect it, you can unintentionally take something home and have a hell of a time breaking that connection.

Take precautions such as simply stating aloud that nobody has your permission to leave with you. Say a prayer as a team, use sage, light a candle, imagine a white light of protection around you, or listen to some Sabbath while inviting beelzebub into your rotting soul! You know, whatever your deal is! Seriously though, you are in command

and need to always remember that. The dangers are real but so are the rewards for communicating with the unseen. I wouldn't trade a single second of any of my experiences, as they collectively have created the man I am today.

THEY HOPPED ON YOUR BACK

'TIL DEATH & BEYOND BY JOHN & STACEY EDWARDS

The Madness of our Method

There are many different types of paranormal investigators. Those, like us, who have had a life changing experience, and the ones who got into the field because they saw it on television. Some investigate because they are intuitive, sensitive, or psychic and feel like they can help the spirits. Some are non-believers because they never experienced anything paranormal, but they would like to. And there are the skeptics, the hardcore debunkers, who investigate to mainly try to find reasons why the activity is *not* paranormal. One thing we all have in common…we want to capture solid, undeniable proof of real paranormal activity.

Believe it or not, capturing evidence on an investigation is not an exact science. I know, shocking, right? Everyone has their own style, based on their belief of the best ways to capture evidence. Things that work for one person may not work for another. Over the years, John and I have gone through many different versions of teams, ideas, and methods. We made mistakes, but learned from them, and finally developed the method we use today.

As a general rule, John and I investigate by ourselves. We started as part of a large team, then we started our own smaller team. Eventually, we ended up with just the two of us, and it works. When there are only two people on an entire location, the atmosphere is much different than having ten people breaking into teams, rotating shifts, and constantly asking where the others are located. We have people we can call to join us if we need them, and we happily join teams that ask us to come along. After all, sharing ideas is important to further the field, but nothing beats being alone in a haunted location with only one other person.

Investigations last more than one night. In order to do a proper investigation, we make it known that we will need more than one night to investigate. If we go to a location and get nothing the first night, it doesn't necessarily mean the place is not haunted. Spirits can hide if they don't want to be discovered. If we investigate three times and get nothing, it is most likely not haunted. On the other hand, if the location is very active and we get EVPs with names or phrases, we can use that information to form the questions for our next investigation. Bottom line, the more time you spend in the same location, the better.

During EVP sessions, we don't ask for specific spirits by name, unless the name comes up in our evidence. Asking for a spirit by a specific name could prevent other spirits from answering. Imagine your name is Tom, and someone comes to your house asking for Larry over and over. Are you going to talk to that person? Probably not. Just because your uncle Fred died in the bedroom a few years ago doesn't necessarily mean he is still there causing activity. If, however, we get the name Fred on an EVP or through the Spirit Box, then we would ask for Fred by name. A spirit can end up in a location for a number of reasons, so it's safer not to assume ahead of time that you know who is there.

Along this same line of thought, whenever possible, we like to do the first investigation blind, or without knowing the history or claims of the location. Just tell us where you feel the hot spots are and we will hear your claims after. That way, if we get evidence, we will look at it objectively and not try to make it fit into a specific story from the history of the location. Then, when we hear the claims and research the history, we can make honest connections to any evidence we collected, or personal experiences we had, and validate them.

During the investigation, trust your feelings and use the equipment to back them up. Over time, the more you investigate, the better you become. If you want to play baseball, and you practice every day, eventually you will get a "feel" for the game and get better. The same applies with the paranormal. You eventually become more and more sensitive to the energies and feelings associated with paranormal activity the more you experience it. John and I rely heavily on this technique.

We go where we feel the activity is happening, then we use our equipment to try to capture evidence to verify what we are feeling. Most investigators have a "tell," or something specific that happens when paranormal activity is close. Sometimes it's the chills, or a headache, or ringing in the ears. For me, I get a queasy, sick feeling. The stronger the energy, the sicker I feel. If I think I am about to throw up, that's when I know I need to turn on my recorder and start asking questions!

Trust your feelings

As far as equipment goes, don't overdo it. Some of our best investigations were done with a recorder and a flashlight. Don't get me wrong, we love our equipment, but you have to have limits. If you have eight DVR cameras, four static cameras, a recorder in every room, laser grids set up, shadow detectors on the stairs, and 16 REM pods lining the hallway while you're holding a thermal camera in one hand and an SLS camera in the other, you should consider scaling it back a bit. Pick one or two items to use at the same time. If those don't work, try a different piece of equipment. If it doesn't work, keep trying different items until you get results. Too much equipment at once can be distracting and actually keep spirits from getting close to you.

Write down or record any personal experiences while you are still on the investigation. I always take time to write down any personal experience that happens, even if it seems unimportant at the time. Memory is a tricky thing, and even though you feel like you won't forget what happened, sometimes the details get fuzzy. In order to record the experience accurately, it should be done while the memory is fresh, and always record every detail. These experiences can be dictated to a digital recorder, typed on your phone, or recorded with a video camera. Personally, I prefer to actually write things down in a journal I keep with me.

Sometimes patterns will emerge from the experiences. We investigated a theater several times over the course of a year. One of my personal experiences was feeling a tingling sensation in my left arm. I noticed that this happened quite a few times. I asked about it during an EVP session once and we captured an EVP saying, "I pulled you." I would never have asked about the tingling if I had not noticed it happening more than once.

We don't dismiss activity simply because it can be debunked. Debunking is the term investigators use when they find a rational reason to explain particular activity. Now, I'm not saying we don't look for a logical explanation for possible paranormal activity, I'm just saying that we don't immediately dismiss activity because there could possibly be another explanation. For example, let's say a client saw a shadow figure in the hallway. It just so happens that if a car drives slowly around the corner on a windy night when the neighbors have their trash cans at the road, it creates a shadow that hits the window and possibly reflects into the hallway. Yes, that is an explanation, and some investigators would say the shadow figure in the hallway was "debunked." When in doubt, throw it out, and all that. But, just because that could possibly be the cause of the shadow figure, it is still entirely possible that there is *actually* a shadow figure in the hallway, and the hallway should still be investigated accordingly.

It's important to take the time to develop your own investigation style. Try new things, be open to change, learn from what doesn't work, and don't think you have to do things exactly the same way as someone else. You may just invent your own technique. This reminds me of a story about John and Tim and their "Scooby-Doo Maneuver."

John and Tim were investigating together at Waverly Hills

Sanatorium. It seemed that whenever John and Tim were together, things happened. Granted, things always happened around John no matter who was with him, but it seemed like Tim was a particularly good trigger for him.

Develop your own style

They were on the first floor and saw a shadow figure. Both turned their flashlights on the figure, and to their surprise, the light did not even penetrate it. Without thinking, they both ran towards the figure. This doesn't seem like a well thought out strategy, but it is nice to know they didn't run *away* from the activity. The shadowy figure ran! They continued to chase it into one of the rooms until Tim stopped short.

"What the hell are we doing? What are we going to do if we catch that thing?" Tim asked.

"I have no idea," John replied. Suddenly a fear gripped them both and they left the area.

Later that night, their testosterone took over and they decided to go back to the first floor and try to at least see the shadow figure again. This particular area was very active. Previously, John and another investigator saw a pair of flesh colored legs running down the hallway!

John suggested they walk down the hall in the dark. It was straight and clear, so there was no possibility of getting hurt. As they were walking, something was following them.

"Hey Tim," John whispered out of the side of his mouth, "do you hear…"

"Yeah, I hear it," Tim whispered back.

"Ok, on the count of three, stop walking. 1…2…3."

They stopped and stood perfectly still. From behind them they heard three more footsteps, then quiet.

Without turning his head, John whispered again, "Start walking again."

They walked a little way and again heard extra footsteps following them.

"On the count of three, stop. 1…2…3."

Again they stopped and stood perfectly still. Again they heard three more footsteps behind them, then quiet.

"I feel like I'm in an episode of Scooby Doo," John exclaimed, still whispering.

"I was thinking the same thing," Tim replied.

"Ok, here's what we are going to do. Let's start walking, and when I say go, we'll spin around and shine our lights on whatever is back there."

They started walking, heard the footsteps following them, John gave the signal, they spun around quickly, and pointed their flashlights at…..nothing. But, the "Scooby-Doo Maneuver" was born and has been used quite a few times since.

•

The Madness of our Method

'Til Death & Beyond by John & Stacey Edwards

A Field Of Theories

The question of what happens after we die is right up there with are we alone in the universe. From the moment we are old enough to think intelligently, we have questions. As many other kids, I was fed the absolute answer according to the church my family attended. There is nothing wrong with people believing in whatever makes them feel better about life and death, but for me, there is a continuation of life in some form after we die.

I have communicated with many spirits of people who were living, breathing human beings at one time. The reason they are still here is the mystery, as well as the question of how many of us stay behind. Does everyone live on after death or do some of us cross over? Why do some decide, or become forced to stick around? It's these questions that drive me to continue this research into the unknown world around us.

The black mass that ran through the house and witnessed by both Stacey and I was all the proof I would ever need. But, in the 20 years since that day, we have found countless hours of audio and video evidence all leading us to where? Well, in my opinion, it has led us closer to an answer, and at the same time has afforded us the wonderful chance of helping many people experiencing paranormal phenomena themselves.

What is a ghost? I've had this question posed to me many times and the answer is simple. If I knew an exact answer then I wouldn't need to burn through hundreds of dollars in batteries a year. There is no exact science to this field, and with that said, there are countless theories and opinions out there. The thoughts I have on the matter are many and have been formed, reformed, tossed aside, and reformed once again as you are always learning and growing. The moment you stop learning is the moment you should probably hang up your Mel-Meter and move on to collecting stamps.

We live in a world where people want their information now! They also want to believe we have a basic understanding of everything. What I believe is, the more I discover, the more questions it always seems to raise. In every type of scientific field the ultimate goal is to prove a theory. The problem with being a researcher of the paranormal is when you actually seem to prove a theory…everything seems to change the next time you investigate.

However, there are many accepted theories and ghost hunter canon that many paranormal investigators treat as holy ground that you should never challenge. One of the most widely accepted theories in the field would be the three major types of hauntings…residual, intelligent, and demonic. Of course it can be broken down to a hundred more classifications, but I like to go with what I have been force-fed the most. I will describe these three classifications and add my personal opinion on one of these in particular.

A residual haunting is supposedly like a tape recorder that plays at a certain time. It always plays the same piece of the past but has no idea that we are around. Some examples of this would be the lonely lady in white staring out to the sea, awaiting the return of her lover. It always seems to be some kind of energy imprint that will forever be trapped. People almost seem let down when you tell them they have some residual activity going on. I have never understood that line of thinking, because just like all other types of hauntings, we are still learning about all of the distinctions that define them.

Residual, to me, is very exciting because the mystery is what exactly causes certain events to be 'trapped'? Is there something we can do to hit the play button whenever we want? Or even hit the record button, for that matter. It is very strange when you step back and try to examine it. In my 20 years of living through severe hauntings, investigating the scariest active locations, and carefully documenting all the evidence with a fine tooth comb…I have found no proof supporting a residual haunting.

I personally believe that when some people pass on they simply keep repeating what they did on a certain day or in a specific place. I believe this happens due to some ghosts being a sort of displaced consciousness and maybe, just maybe, they remember their room, their house, or even their entire neighborhood street. It becomes their construct inside of this prison of an unconscious consciousness, so to speak. Everything I just described would explain many hauntings we refer to as "residual," because we see the white lady walking to the window, seemingly unaware of our presence.

The thing is, I believe it's many times a simple mimicking of a very common human type behavior of denial. Somewhere in the back of their spiritual mind, they don't accept that they're dead. They keep living out these moments to prevent the pain and agony of accepting the sobering truth. Seems pretty human to me, and that is what we believe these residual hauntings to actually be.

Keep looking for answers

I believe that sometimes we just happen to do something rather interesting and honestly terrifying. What if every one of these ghosts are indeed intelligent? And what if we accidentally just so happen to wake them up from their eternal time loop? Perhaps this would explain the desperation or anger we capture in so many EVP's. Maybe I'm just lucky (or even just cursed), but whenever I've been on an investigation where paranormal activity is reported (even residual activity), I have always received intelligent type responses via recordings, or physical activity such as knocks when attempting to communicate.

Now, in no way, shape, or form am I saying this is an absolute truth. It's simply one of so many theories. The exciting part of this field is you are allowed and encouraged to form your own theories and opinions. Test others theories, share your own, and continue to develop your communication styles based on what you have learned along the way.

An intelligent haunting can have many sub-categories attached to its description. An intelligent spirit realizes we are around. It may try to communicate with you or even show its intelligence by preferring to stay away from human contact at all costs. Just like you and me, there are nice spirits and there are evil, or, at the very least, negative ones.

The reason for these spirits to still be around is the question it seems that they, themselves, don't even have an answer for. In the past, I have captured hundreds of "help me" EVPs. Why do these spirits need our help? It's a scary thought that we may die and then be trapped in some building and nobody can explain to us why. For every "help me" it also seems I catch a "get out" or "leave now." The reason for these more negative responses is also a mystery. I have captured thousands of EVP's over the years and sometimes you can piece together the evidence to create a story that is almost never all sunshine and rainbows.

A demonic or inhuman haunting is a controversial topic and supposedly a very rare occurrence. The inhuman part of it is actually an incredibly large spectrum of possibilities. Inhuman, by its pure definition, would simply describe paranormal activity not associated with a deceased human being. We could be dealing with one of the many different and well documented cases of elemental, little people, fairies, etc. Stacey and I actually believe in this side of the paranormal more heavily than many others, due to some personal experiences in the field.

A true demonic haunting is another beast altogether. At one point I honestly wanted to only pursue possible demonic cases. It was during a particularly dark time for me personally, that in hindsight, I can see very clearly why this may have occurred. We are one hundred percent sure that we suffered from demonic oppression while living in the Black House - which we'll visit soon.

A demonic oppression is when a negative presence is in your life but absolutely not making itself known. Rather, so many things start going wrong in your world. Your relationships start to suffer, you may feel withdrawn, paranoid that everyone is against you, become sick most of the time, and honestly ponder things that normally would never cross your mind. Imagine you're playing a video game and turn your luck attribute down to zero…the bad guy works on corrupting you and beating you the hell down until you are primed for an actual possession.

There is nothing romantic or exciting about the negative variety of hauntings. Some people screw around with the dark for power or knowledge. Others just do it because they have very bad intentions and want to strike a curse on someone. If I'm ever serious about something it would be the fact that this is all real. It can most definitely hurt you or the ones you care about.

Stacey and I came up with the idea of recreating the famous Scole Experiment, which was documented in a 90's era British documentary. The gist of the idea is to gather a group of sensitives together in a controlled environment and attempt seance communication with the other side week after week, at the same place, and at the same time. The results do indeed get stronger each and every week, but you truly need to be aware of who you conduct any experiment like this with.

We participated in the experiment for probably a month's worth of sessions. What ended up happening was things we didn't like, and it was absolutely affecting the others far worse than it was us. Not our first rodeo at all, and we were luckily able to see warning signs of people enjoying a certain feeling of power. It was a long time ago and probably belongs in our "mistakes" chapter, if it belongs anywhere at all. The end result was very negative for some of the participants, but luckily not us, due to us having the presence of mind to step away.

Residual, intelligent, inhuman, or anything associated with the paranormal field, all have to be approached with respect and with a healthy dose of caution. It's not all lollipops and unicorns like you may think from watching your tv Ghost Busters. Long before the human race even kept decent records, we were communicating with the spiritual world, feeling it's energies and powers, and paying the price for carelessness.

I can think of case after case that the same patterns seem to appear. The patterns I'm referring to is my team going into the location and getting great evidence, then all of a sudden it stops. We will go from getting EMF interaction or knocks when asking for it to absolutely nothing.

Now, I'm sure some of you will point out that spirits use energy to interact with us and maybe after some communicating they are spent. Well, I also think that's possible and a very good theory. But it seems a lot of the time something else altogether is afoot at these locations.

I think that some of these places are ruled, so to speak, by one stronger, negative entity who keeps these other spirits almost locked up. Now, is this always the case? No. But in countless locations we have seen evidence of this. We have even asked questions about it and received answers on EVP leaning that way. This particular theory is the one that probably haunts me more than any other theory I have developed. I have a name for it and will now share that name, that theory, and a few of my other favorite theories of the many I have created over the course of twenty years.

A Field Of Theories

On the search

THE KEEPER THEORY

After spending many years in the paranormal field, you will develop theories based on what you have observed along the way. I know that, personally, I have grown to see the paranormal phenomena in a much different light than many other researchers. In this chapter, I will be discussing something Stacey and I have come to call "The Keeper."

It all started a few years back during one of our overnight investigations of the notorious Waverly Hills Sanatorium in Louisville, Kentucky. Tina Matherly, the world's most awesome Haunted Attraction owner, was showing us some pictures captured from the security cameras on the front gate. The pictures displayed what can be described in no other way than as an intelligent spirit jailbreak attempt.

There was an orb (a ball of possible spirit energy) that approached the gate like it was trying to leave the grounds. When it reached the front gate, there was another piece of energy spotted that took the form of a cloaked apparition. It seemed to gather the first orb and return it inside.

Now, before everyone starts screaming "That was dust following dust into the desert of dust-opia," let me quickly state this theory is not based in the slightest on the footage I'm speaking of, orbs, dust, nor any other visual evidence to speak of. The foundations are comprised of a solid bit of audio evidence we have collected over the years.

In ghost hunting, you will run across a number of big buildings that are, for all intents and purposes, vacant. They may have been hospitals, factories, or even former mansions that are now in disrepair. Most all of the time with these bigger venues there will be quite a large number of recorded or rumored deaths associated with said property.

My teams and I have always rather enjoyed these bigger structures because of the opportunity for true research and experiments. In a building with numerous floors, you can possibly find multiple types of hauntings at the same location. Waverly Hills, for instance, is like the Wal-Mart of paranormal research. The Hill has everything from a jilted lover to a reported doppelgänger.

It was at one of these bigger locations that I first stumbled on the idea of the keeper. In late 2006, we were called to investigate a place called Beehive Antiques, in the quiet little town of Elizabethton, TN. The building had served as a clinic decades earlier and had rumors of a dark past.

Before the new owners renovated the building into an antique shop, the building had been vacant for a number of years. You will find this to be the case with many larger locations. If the paranormal boom has accomplished anything, the community can boast the fact that it has restored many decrepit buildings to their former glory.

At the Beehive, we recorded dozens of class A intelligent EVPs and all had great personal experiences to boot. The one thing I began to notice with the evidence was that we would be getting great interaction with a spirit, only to have it shut down soon after, feeling a dark, heavy, and even oppressive weight seemingly enter the room.

As with anything, this went unnoticed the first few times it occurred. In hindsight, the phenomena had occurred at almost every larger location I had investigated. Almost like a warden or a "keeper" of the other, weaker spirits, it knows when they are communicating with us and somehow wants interaction to come to a halt.

It was merely a point of speculation when I first began to see the string of events unfolding. An investigator would be having an incredible session that may have included EMF spikes on command, intelligently controlled temperature drops, or even disembodied voices. Then, for reasons unknown, the activity would cease.

There is, of course, the argument of the energy a spirit uses to actively communicate with us diminishing. After which, the activity would obviously lighten, or end completely. I don't argue with that at all because it is nothing short of a recorded fact. The thing I am talking about is going from turning a flashlight on and off on command, and then nothing at all except a passing heavy feeling. This chain of events has happened in varying ways to me many times.

The first audio evidence of this came during an investigation of a nearly 100 year old former bank building. The building was three floors of activity with a basement that still haunts me to this very day. The second floor had an apartment where the word heavy isn't heavy enough. When I walked in, I could feel the presence of a strong and anxious spirit. Most of the time, if you are sensitive like me or not, anyone can feel the presence of an anxious spirit while you are dialed in to your senses.

After the better part of an hour inside that apartment with my longtime partner Tim and my wife, Stacey, the room got a crazy vibe and then...nothing. Upon later review, some amazing EVPs were discovered occurring during that same time.

The first were of a female who was answering our questions on command. This was followed by a nasty sounding male who was captured on a fantastic piece of audio, interrupting the female voice with a strong *"Shut Up."* Then, while Tim and Stacey were taking a series of photos, the male once again chimed in with a *"turn that camera off."*

That place was investigated at a very odd time for me personally, and whatever the keeper of the building was up to, he did a number on me by the time the end of the night came. I ended up being drawn back into this building too many times. Even though we think an investigation has to have more than one visit, it can also get out of hand.

The EVP showing the interaction between the two spirits was indeed a solid bit of support to the keeper theory. The next bit of evidence, however, was about to blow the lid off of everything I had been working on. And it was going to come to us at a movie theater of all places.

In 2010 and 2011, we investigated an independently owned movie theater in eastern Tennessee. The owners wanted it investigated due to the employees experiencing what seemed like nonstop activity. We started looking for innocent children ghosts, per the claims, and ended up with the birth of "the keeper."

After the first investigation covered the seven theaters and the projection room, we saw, felt, and heard an unbelievable amount of activity. But this place was falling straight in line with the "great activity that is quickly suppressed" problem. By this point I was already suspecting that a great number of larger venues were watched over by a keeper of sorts, so I dissected the evidence with a fine toothed comb. There were many sessions where an investigator was getting great interaction and then the answers would stop or an angry voice would show up.

The most awesome of these was an EVP I will forever keep close to me. I was asking about who was angry with us, who attacked a fellow investigator, and so on. As you can tell by my line of questioning, this was a crazy night indeed. As we were heading into the darkest theater, Theater Seven, the EVP in question was captured stating *"The Keeper Will."* This EVP, by itself, means very little. But, with everything that had been occurring inside this building, it ignited a spark inside my mind.

The name "The Keeper" is obviously not some universally accepted and known phrase taught to all freshly deceased spirits. You're more than likely not going to be able to go into an investigation and ask for the keeper and expect the ghosts to be like "Oh, crap…You caught us." It's a name I captured on EVP that those particular spirits used to refer to the oppressive spirit that kept them from intelligently communicating with the freaks who talk to themselves in dark rooms.

Be it the keeper, the boss, the bright man, or the almighty reaper of eternal sorrow, the name doesn't matter nearly as much as the act itself. The same pattern of control has seemed to occur at countless— and I do mean countless—locations that we have investigated over the years.

One controlling spirit, human or otherwise, has some sinister secret, in some cases, or has a role to play that involves public relations for the other side. Some places, where there was a high number of deaths due to fatal illnesses, could have someone who perhaps made a last-second deal with the departed.

Whatever the reasons behind "the keeper," the fact remains I have seen firsthand that in many large buildings with a high number of ghosts as residents, there is almost always a leader. And this leader is rarely open for anything other than wanting us to leave.

The Keeper theory is just that, a theory. This is a field built on and defined by speculation and theories. Even the methods we use to communicate with spirits are, in essence, only theories themselves.

When we stop exploring new theories and inhibit igniting thoughts in others minds to develop, then we may as well give it all up.

So, the next time you and your team are on location in an old hospital, medieval castle, or southern movie theater, just remember if you have a great session suddenly go cold…the keeper may be putting the kibosh on your paranormal pajama party. Explore the unknown and expand on this and other theories for yourself.

'Til Death & Beyond by John & Stacey Edwards

Pay Per Boos

After so many years of living, breathing, eating, and sleeping the paranormal, you tend to learn a thing or two. As I, and so many other longtime investigators always proclaim: "This is not an exact science." That's not to say that there can't be a few tried and true practices that can directly impact your ability to conduct a solid investigation.

I have quite a few theories I have developed over the years, all arising directly from experiences. Everything from investigation etiquette to successful evidence review. As with any other job, with experience comes knowledge. What may begin as what you have seen others do or say will quickly turn and evolve into your own practices.

I intend on exploring most, if not all, of my main theories within the pages of this book. In no way, shape, or form would I expect someone to adopt these theories and instantly expect incredible results. I can guarantee, however, that you may end up reading something I have personally discovered and be like "Holy crap! That's what happened to my team." I hope some of these experiences will somehow work to help another team facing similar circumstances.

Ok, so picture this, and let me know if it sounds familiar. You, and your team of fearless ghost chasing superstars have been super jacked up about an upcoming investigation at an über-excelente locale. Hundreds of dollars in extra batteries have been purchased, hotel points have been cashed in at the Days Inn, hundreds of pictures of the location have been successfully shared on Facebook, and somebody's cousin talked a fireman out of a thermal camera for a night. All your bases are indeed covered for a spectacular investigation.

Upon arriving at said castle of creepy dreams, you unpack and set up for your research into the unknown to begin. The thing is, the trip itself kind of stretched your finances a little, or your significant other perhaps woke up on the wrong side of the bed again this morning. Right now, you could care less because you are where you want to be, doing what you feel you were born to do…What could go wrong?

The hours start passing and you begin to get frustrated because not so much as a mouse fart has been heard thus far. This place is supposed to cause people to start spitting up pea soup on nearby padres! It's a place where that thin veil between worlds seems to vanish. It's the Walt Disney world of paranormal destinations, and yet nothing is going on except your blood pressure rising.

Things are being made worse because your tech assistant has a friend of his boss's cousin who once saw an episode of Paranormal State and decided to chip in and experience some ghosts for himself. You know the great evidence your team always gets, but nothing seems to be going on here. You increase your question volume and even begin to leave your comfort zone by using provocation.

After ten minutes in a room without having a ghost finish your "Shave and a Haircut" routine, you declare this room to not be hot with activity right now and decide to move on. In the next room, not one single spirit decided to turn on your flashlight! This is getting ridiculous! Then, to make matters worse, your iPhone goes off with a text from your mother reminding you about how God feels about ghost hunting. This is truly a lost cause and you decide to call it quits early because it just isn't charged tonight.

Unfortunately, thanks to the wonders of "wham bam, thank you ma'am" paranormal television programming, many new investigators have nights that play out just like this. What they fail to realize is that paranormal activity is an elusive phenomena that it is pretty dang rare to experience, at least on command or in large doses, that is. A paranormal investigation should be entered into free of outside manipulations. You have to clear your mind of all of life's continuous stressful nuggets of anxiety.

Another problem that many people rarely understand until it's pointed out is that having a guest investigator with you can be horrific. A good team knows each other's sniffs, spits, whispers, and feelings. Even if said guest remains super silent for the duration of the investigation, he/she can still unintentionally screw up your evidence because you don't know their sounds.

When someone new is with you, it is human nature to want to show them your skills. The problem with this is the age old issue of trying too hard. You know better than anyone that your best evidence may require eight hours of absolute boring silence. Aside from a rabid bat or a loose floor board, many times it's next to impossible to judge the success of an investigation based solely on personal experiences.

The example I gave you was that of what I like to refer to as "Pay Per Boos." Those magnificent, grandiose, ancient structures which have been featured on your favorite Hollywood movie or ghost hunting show. By the time you get there you have paid God knows how much on the eight hour overnight property rental, hotel rooms, rental cars, restaurants, etc. You're expecting something big and something quick because you saw Zak piss his pants on the third floor only 14 minutes into the show.

What you may fail to realize is that many of the most popular paranormal shows spend more than one night at the location. Or that scene from 14 minutes into the show was actually after 11 hours of investigating. These are only a few of the factors that cause a condition I like to refer to as "paranormal fatigue," It can be caused by any number of outside stressful factors in your life.

You can have the most incredible investigation of your life just as easily at a local residential as you can at a 100 year old prison for pet molesters. Spirits are indeed everywhere and could care less whether you are using the Ovilus Extreme GT 3000 or a 20 year old Kodak and cassette recorder. It's not the location or the equipment that brings out the spirit. It's the circumstances trapping this poor soul here on earth and the dedication of your research that matters.

Please don't misunderstand me, because I love going to Waverly Hills (and other such places) more than most, I promise. I even enjoy the vacation aspect of traveling to these beautiful and historic locations. The problem is, you are not going to unlock the eternal secrets of the afterlife under stressful conditions in an eight hour window of playtime. Now, you can most definitely obtain incredible evidence during this time, but treat it as you would a vacant building in your own neighborhood. Follow your same protocols and procedures and don't enter in with Hollywood expectations. I guarantee you'll enjoy your evening 100 percent better.

It's always important to never enter any kind of paranormal

investigation while under any kind of emotional stress. A broken relationship, an addictive habit, and even a bad day at work can all leave you vulnerable to an attack. The darker spirits seem to feed off of these emotional issues like ice cream in the Mojave Desert.

Unfortunately, I only speak about this from personal experiences. I have been through pure Hell at more than one time in my life. Each time it happened, it began with me entering into the investigation while at a very low point in my personal life.

The research of the paranormal can be extremely rewarding for those who want to help someone else. It can also be rewarding for those of us that want to continue to find answers to life's most mysterious questions regarding what happens next. But if its thrill seeking and table tipping you're searching for, I'm afraid you'll become disheartened very early on in your career. Just keep an open, objective mind and steer clear of Hollywood expectations.

The main part of my "Pay Per Boos" is that we only began seeing people pay to investigate these places after the great ghost rush boom of 2005. Day after day, night after night, year after year, you have 300 plus days a year of different teams, every night, putting all of their energy into these locations.

The problem with this is some of these people are taking serious emotional problems in with them. Some take dark intentions, some take innocent excitement, and others are trying to have serious research conducted. It's a melting pot of energies all feeding into these spirits. Spirits who, from all we have ascertained, are big bundles of energy attached to some form of consciousness. See the potential issue here kiddos? Either we are going to affect them or they are going to affect us. And to what end?

The answer is that we really don't know yet. The data simply isn't complete concerning what has changed in every major Hollywood Haunt Pay Per Boo out there.

What was that? Examples you say? Sure, I'll give you a good one my friends! Back to good ol' Waverly Hills. When I first went to Waverly a decade ago, it was scary yet rather tame. I experienced activity and nothing dark or menacing save the gosh darned 4th floor of impending doom (see The Keeper chapter.)

The next time I went? Well, there was a black dog we witnessed running on the ceiling. You know normal paranormal progression right? And the next? Well, the next time started with a warning of a possible doppelgänger?! Yes, that escalated quickly!

Is this because of my theory being accurate? Well, probably yes, but we truly can't say that just yet. Now, if next year we hear the Winchesters were seen running from the building, arms flailing, while sucking on their pacifiers...maybe we should start a paranormal vetting process.

Look, it's a field of theories as I've said a million times. This is just one of mine that I truly believe in. So keep your third eye open to this and all possibilities, because you are helping write the canon yourselves each time you get your gear and enter a haunted building.

'Til Death & Beyond   by John & Stacey Edwards

THE THEORY OF FEAR

Everything is made up of energy, and I truly believe everything is connected in the universe. Sometimes it seems when we put out positive energy, we receive that same positivity back. Of course, it works the same way with negative emotions and energy. I feel this is an easy way to explain karma that I have seen work nearly everyday of my life in some shape or form.

I also tend to believe these floating balls of consciousness we call ghosts are made up of energy as well. I think the difference with the ghosts is they don't have rechargeable batteries like the ones of us still hanging out in our meat suits. When a soul leaves the body it seems they require a certain amount of charging in order to communicate with us effectively.

Whenever you're on an investigation and the batteries in your flashlight die or the camera goes belly up, and you absolutely know you had just changed every single one of them before you started, it's because the ghosts you are attempting to chat with are sucking energy from wherever they can get it.

With those of us still living, we have energy in abundance to communicate at will because of our inner bits (actual medical terminology.) Our floating friends, however, need a constant string of big-belly battery burgers to keep up your intriguing line of "what is your name?" and "Why are you here?" questions. (Side note: I always imagine a ghost standing there like Samuel L. Jackson responding with "WHAT THE F@&K IS YOUR NAME M*#HER$U&@ER!!")

For some ghosts though, it sometimes seems like we unintentionally open ourselves up to giving too much of our own energy. There have been many times that my team and I have felt like we just ran a marathon in Kathmandu after an hour inside of a building. It's a rare occurrence but it has happened.

One place that sticks out like a sore thumb is the Old South Pittsburg Hospital in South Pittsburg, Tennessee. That place and I have a hate hate type relationship stemming from my trips to the home of our spiritual energy vampires. Every time my team and I walked inside the doors of the former hospital, we experienced emotional and physical breakdowns. The first time we were there it just didn't make much sense to us as to why we were all so dead tired and useless.

Discussing the investigation plan at Old South

The Theory Of Fear

The second time we went, we were filming a full fledged documentary and broadcasting live on the internet for a 24 hour live investigation. Within the first hour we were already beginning to splinter. Our team was already trimmed down by that point and were like family.

I seemed to be the most susceptible to the attack. The thing I've been told about myself is that how ever John goes, so does everyone else in the room with him. If I'm happy, everybody's happy! If I'm stressing out, everybody is a walking car crash. I still think my empathic abilities just pick up on everyone else and then it becomes magnified through my own manifestation of that emotion. Regardless, this place was playing us like a Stradivarius!

The activity was sneaky in the building as well. You didn't really know you were being messed with until it was too late. The ghosts in that place aren't really the "Shave and a Haircut" variety whatsoever. They hide and follow you, just sucking up whatever energy you're putting out. This is where I first thought up my idea for the "Go Dark" experiment.

The "Go Dark" experiment is based off of the assumption that ghosts rely on energy, and the more energy we are putting out, the higher the levels of activity we will experience from the ghost. I believe that when our heart rate increases, our anxiety shoots sky high, and for lack of a better word, we become afraid that a ghost will feed off of that energy.

When we attempt this experiment, we ensure that the Stacey is perfectly safe! (I mean come on! I have to use Stacey because we all know I would never show fear!) All joking aside, the subject going dark will be in a room alone, no walkie, no LED screen, no flashlight. We monitor the IR video and listen to the audio while the subject starts to deal with being alone inside of a dark and haunted room.

Regardless of what we show on the outside, it's a perfectly natural reaction to experience increased levels of your senses while sitting in a dark and unfamiliar room. The results of this experience have been incredible every time we attempted it.

The one that comes to mind instantly is from the Major Graham Mansion, in which I stuffed Stacey inside a closet where activity had always been reported. I was on the other side of the door and she was absolutely calm, brave, and willing to do whatever it took to score some awesome evidence. What she captured was immediate and intelligent responses that we were all able to hear as it happened. "Is there anyone in here with me?" *"I'm in here with you"*...so creepy.

Discussing the investigation plan at Old South

If we are all energy and "if" ghosts require ample amounts of energy, it only makes sense that when we increase our output the interactions also increase in power. Think back to when you had some of your best interactions. For us, a lot of times it's been when we were all huddled up like the Scooby gang walking down a hallway. As I constantly remind everyone, this is but a theory and so is this beautiful field of paranormal research.

Next time you and your team find yourselves more interested in sitting at home base watching monitors, rather than going back to the third floor, you may just be experiencing a siphoning of your energy reserves due to Vlad the unseen Casper! And maybe, just maybe it's time for you to Go Dark!

The Theory Of Fear

'Til Death & Beyond by John & Stacey Edwards

Electronic Summonings

My eyes were bloodshot and dried out from the five plus hours of evidence review. Those nights when Stacey had to close at her job were always the best for knocking out some audio review. My bedroom door was closed and I had my best headphones on as I sat cross legged and stared blankly at the ceiling.

With eyes wide open, I didn't see the ceiling at all. I only saw the Old Sullivan County Bank Building in Downtown Kingsport, Tennessee. We had become veterans of the historical downtown buildings in Kingsport after investigating several in a short span of time. The entire city seems to be haunted, and strangely connected by some invisible thread. I truly believe that somehow the connection lay beneath the structures. Regardless, the particularly intense Bennett and Edwards building (formally Sullivan County Bank Building) had given not only me but many others some fits.

We had a man from the local newspaper embedded with us for a feature story on our local paranormal team. He lasted about five minutes with me in the basement. The activity was "on command" for me! But there was much more than just an active location to this place.

I had previously captured an EVP Stating *"I wish I could kill him"* from a female in the basement. It was heavy…just very dark and heavy on my chest, my mind, and my soul. I was not at my highest point when we first investigated and I'm pretty confident I was open for attacks.

For these obvious reasons, I was incredibly tense during this particular audio review session. Every step, every breath, every whisper were all being played back in my mind's eye as I followed along with the audio. I only stopped to cut out and save any possible voices.

As I got to a point where we were on the 2nd floor in the

banquet room, I heard a very menacing and foretelling voice talking about being attached to me.

While I was envisioning this occurrence in my crystal clear memory, I started feeling cold and nervous. The very unusual feeling of fear inside the safety of my own bedroom was quickly descending on me. I quit replaying this selection and took off my headphones to find a room that was almost too silent.

The next series of events happened so fast that it took my mind hours to truly start making any type of sense of what happened. All of a sudden, I felt a rush of air hit my face, I heard a very loud bang come from all around me, and I heard my name said in the completely disembodied voice of a female. I now think the female voice was a warning and unrelated to the bang and the air blast, but nonetheless some very strange events had just happened inside of my otherwise not-haunted home.

It didn't happen again for about a year, as I was once again reviewing audio from the Major Graham Mansion inside a completely new house. The stories from Graham Mansion are for another time. I could fill an entire series of books with how that house has affected my personal life.

This time was very similar because I always review audio the same way. I retrace my actions, picture the hallways, rooms, smells, sounds, and tastes of where I was when recording the audio. This fact is very important to what I am proposing here.

Something happened to me that night that I still can't fully explain. While reviewing the audio, I started seeing flashes of light inside my downstairs bedroom. I knew I was alone at the time as Stacey and the kids were all upstairs hanging out.

I don't remember any temperature flux or anything other than an odd feeling that I was looking down at myself on the bed. The very next thing I knew I was sitting in the upstairs living room floor! Stacey had a notebook with many words written down in a very frantic style of writing.

Stacey appeared to be in that freaked-out-fake-calm way that she appears when crap has just hit the fan. She can maintain a high degree of calm and dignity through the most dire of circumstances. I've been with her for half of my life, so I know when she is upset or excited in any way. She was upset and excited on this night, on that floor, in front of her husband.

I'm not going to present a full play by play of what happened because I don't wish to sensationalize this strange and very personal event. I will just say that someway or somehow I opened myself up to the other side unintentionally. It felt new but it also felt all too familiar.

That's when it hit me like a ton of bricks! Everything seemed to fill with color inside of a black and white dream. The audio review was somehow opening a door to not only the other side…it was opening a door inside of the location I was reviewing! Many other less significant events that occurred during audio evidence review started flashing back to me like lost memories being recalled by an alien abductee.

I was creating some kind of electronic summoning from the spirits inside of these buildings. As fantastic as it sounds to even me, it's really the only thing that actually makes some kind of sense. I firmly believe anything can be used to communicate with the dead. You don't have to have a 100 year old spirit board on a full moon to open up the veil and more so, just open up yourself.

Somehow, I was becoming a conduit to these spirits while completely reconstructing their locations. I was placing myself inside of these places in a true and deep meditative state. Everything lined up to the why it could happen, if not the how.

I do believe that "theory" is a strong word for this one, as I would refer to it more as a hypothesis: "a supposition or proposed explanation made on the basis of limited evidence as a starting point for further investigation." Which seems to make more sense to me at this point. As with many parts of the paranormal, ufology, cryptozoology, and just the strange…more research is truly required to move these "ideas" forward into the light of day.

I know many of you review hour upon countless hour of audio evidence. Just remember next time you're all alone, zoned out, and creating a construct of your investigation location inside your mind, you are also possibly opening up an electronic summoning.

That Darn Cat

I have a particular affinity for animals. John always says if there is a stray animal anywhere near our house, it will find it's way to our door. He always thought I should have a pet of my own, so a year or so after we were married, he bought me a cat. A large Maine Coon, black and white, that I named Mulder. He was a quirky sort of cat who did really unusual things, so he fit right into our family. Most of the time he would follow me around the house, so I was used to having him at my feet.

Sadly, we ended up moving into a place that did not allow pets, and we sent him to live with another family. This is when an odd thing started happening, at least this is when I started noticing it happening. I would be standing in the kitchen or sitting on the couch and see a quick, black flash out of the corner of my eye, close to the floor. I had seen this before, but I always assumed it was the cat, since he was almost always at my feet. However, I was still seeing it, even after the cat was gone.

I didn't mention anything about this to John. I thought maybe my eyes were just playing tricks on me, or maybe I just missed the cat so much I was still seeing him. One night I was making dinner, and John was in the kitchen with me. I saw the black flash near the floor, and turned my head to look in the direction I saw it. John saw me look, and incredibly he said, "Did you just see that black thing?" Apparently, he had been seeing it too, and also failed to mention it. We both had thought we were just going crazy.

I mentioned in a previous chapter about how we would do investigations, and inadvertently end up bringing all kinds of things home with us. These particular paranormal hitchhikers we were seeing are what we call "astral critters." These critters are small, non-human entities that, for whatever reason, attach themselves to you and follow you home. They appear as small black shadows often seen out of the corner of your eye, near the floor, and generally move quickly out of sight. Mostly the entities are just curious, or they like to play tricks and cause trouble. Perhaps you hear a strange knocking in the middle of the night, or the lights start flickering, or maybe your television will turn on and off by itself randomly. If you start having spurts of activity after spending hours in a haunted location, you may have attracted a critter.

There is another name for these small, playful creatures. They are often referred to as goblins, fairies, pixies, or other similar elemental spirits. Although most people think these creatures are simply fantasy and folklore, this is not the case. Wee folk have been around much longer than humans, and I dare say, they will be around long after. There are many different types of elementals, or nature spirits. The ones we refer to as astral critters are normally the more playful, mischievous types. They like to cause trouble and play pranks, delighting in their ability to startle humans with their antics. Normally, these particular entities will only stick around for a week or two before moving on.

After doing some research on this phenomena, I became particularly fascinated with elemental spirits. Every culture in the world has a story and name for the ancient little beings that inhabit their lands. In Iceland, it's the Huldufolk, Ireland has its leprechauns. In England there are brownies and Germanic folklore speaks of Elves. The Menehune are found in the Hawaiian Islands, the Aziza live in Africa and you could fill an entire book with the different names given to the little people by Native American tribes. There are so many stories from every culture about elementals that I find it amazing how easily their existence is dismissed as nonsense. Tell a skeptic you have a ghost in your house, and they will most likely laugh it off. Tell them you have leprechauns or fairies living in your house or yard, and they will give you "the look." You know, the "I'm pretty sure you have completely lost your mind" look.

Not every country is like this, however. Places like Ireland and Iceland still hold a great respect for the little people. In fact, in Iceland, the government will redirect roads and other major projects if their plans disrupt the Huldufolk in some way. There are still plenty of people who believe enough to put out fairy houses or special tributes of food and items for any visiting elemental spirits.

Leaving offerings out for the elementals

I read a book once called *Summer With the Leprechauns,* by Tanis Helliwell. The book is a true account of a summer the author spent in Ireland, where she met and communed with a leprechaun. I enjoyed the story so much, it inspired me to believe more in the existence of nature spirits and elementals. I started leaving out small tributes of food and tea and offered an open invitation to any and all elementals that were good natured and wished to stay in our home when they passed through the area. The invitation was very specific, as I didn't want to unintentionally invite any of the tricksters or trouble makers. I also vowed to pay attention to the nature around me and the impact I may have on it. I put bird feeders in the yard and tried to be more conscious of the trees, plants, and animals that lived around the house.

An interesting thing has happened in the five years since I started with the offerings. Our home has felt lighter, happier, and maybe a bit more magical. Good things started happening for us. We have not had to deal with any "astral critters" running around. Perhaps it is because I have been putting some positive energy out into the universe, and getting the same in return. Could it be we have had some special visitors that accepted my invitation? I don't know. I don't claim to be able to see or communicate with such beings. But I do believe they are real, and I do believe they appreciate our belief and the small tokens we may leave out for them.

THAT DARN CAT

'Til Death & Beyond by John & Stacey Edwards

Chasing Newport

I can't believe it's been ten long and eventful years since the last time I stepped foot inside this building. In the span of a decade, I investigated the most haunted and well known building on the East Coast of the United States. In all of those hundreds of investigations, I would always tell other investigators about this one place that truly rocked me to my core. In those ten years I was like a junkie trying to chase his greatest high. In ten years I always felt I was chasing Newport.

The course of events that led me to be back in this parking lot across from the Cocke County War Memorial Building in Newport, Tennessee are a strange brew all by themselves. I had been asked to come and film an episode of the hit TLC paranormal show "Ghost Brothers" and to tell my story.

The Ghost Brothers Call

The crazy part about all of this is the synchronicity of it all. Bonita from Pilgrim Films called me to be the guest investigator for an episode at the Major Graham Mansion in Max Meadows, Virginia. I had filmed a documentary at the mansion a few years before and honestly have some serious history with that location.

I felt the spirits in the Graham Mansion didn't want me to return due to some truth I was trying to divulge about some of the former residents. Stacey and I had a hard time even driving by the area of the mansion in recent years. The other crazy part to all of this is the fact we now live in Augusta Maine!

I told Stacey that I felt something would happen before I ever got a chance to return to Graham Mansion. That "something" did in fact happen, and the location fell through without much explanation as to why. Bonita, who may be the hardest working person I've ever met aside from Stacey and I, was devastated for it falling through. She truly wanted to have John Edwards on her show, and more for John Edwards than for Bonita or the Brothers.

Bonita asked me if I had another location that I had a story with, if I knew of a location that had never been on television before. A location that was truly haunted. It took me all of ten minutes before I called her back with a location that I felt may be impossible to actually secure. But a location that had never once left my thoughts since investigating it in 2004 and 2006.

The Cocke County War Memorial in Newport, Tennessee is located in the heart of Newport. It's a small city of 7,000 residents and located on the Pigeon River. The history of the land is as gruesome and bloody as it gets in the history of the U.S., as the great Cherokee Warpath went right through what is now known as Newport.

I have Cherokee blood in my veins and truly feel a certain uneasy feeling when reading about the events of the late 1700's in this area. Nonstop attacks on settlers of the area by Cherokee Natives and the British helped to soak the soil in buckets of innocent blood. The spot the war memorial is built on no doubt has quite a bit of history beneath its foundation.

The thing about the building that stands out to me is the fact there are no documented deaths inside of the actual building. The dark history arises from the housing of the remains from a tragic plane crash back in 1964. It just so happened that the first time I investigated the building it was 40 years after the events of that tragedy.

United Air Flight 823 bound for Knoxville, Tennessee from Washington D.C. exploded in 1964 killing all 39 people aboard the plane. The eyewitness accounts and the events that happened in the wake of the crash are all very suspicious. The cause for the crash is unknown to this day and the plane actually vanished from radar for ten minutes before reappearing, only to apparently catch fire and nose dive into a very remote area. One witness claims a man tried jumping before the crash, but he also perished.

The passengers on the plane included a young boy and girl, several "blood" doctors, and many normal everyday people. The FBI became involved after the crash and retrieved documents found at the scene concerning the Oak Ridge Nuclear Facility near Knoxville. Sound like a classic X-Files episode? Just you wait!

When I investigated this building the first time I had been on many investigations but never with this particular group of people. I don't like doing anything with people I don't have a bond with, so this was very much out of my comfort zone. I tell you though, something has been eating at me about this investigation for years.

The night of the original investigation we all left the building different than we were when we entered. We experienced a high level of PK (psychokinetic) activity, EVPs of a woman screaming for her child, another saying *"I was effin' murdered,"* dark feelings, a slamming door that had been previously locked then slammed open so hard it chipped the wall!

I would say the strangest thing that happened to me that first night occurred in the gymnasium area. That's where old fashioned wooden bingo balls flew at us from nowhere! I know how it sounds, but it truly happened. We heard them rolling on the floor to us even after rolling them away. Later on, a leader of that team figured out that they spelled out boy and girl when using the numbers on the balls. It was heavy.

Let me break this down for a moment. Sometimes when I'm reading or listening to someone else's personal experiences, it's very difficult to actually put myself inside of their experience correctly. It's hard to actually feel the emotions they had coursing through their veins at that moment in time. To be frank, we just hear this stuff and kind of pass it off due to the absolute overload of information coming at us these days.

Back in the early days of the "paranormal boom," as I like to refer to the time that Ghost Hunters first hit the airwaves, the people could hear an EVP of a garbled ghost gasp and be truly screwed up for days. As with anything, you become desensitized to just exactly how freaking insane it is that we are legitimately communicating with unseen entities residing behind a veil of mysterious questions.

I remember that night like it was literally last night. The door slamming moment had already occurred not once but twice. The disembodied voices, the attacks in the basement, it was just heavy man…it wasn't right. It was truly like a dream state we were all sucked into, a group of young investigators who had never worked together before being bathed in a trial by fire. I don't care to admit I was overwhelmed. But, because of the events that Stacey and I had been through, it was almost like I knew what that feeling represented.

So again, there were three of us who decided to walk back into the gymnasium to try and communicate with this powerful spirit who slammed the doors. I was apprehensive, yet excited as could be to hear the doors slam once again. Instead, this time I was hit by a wooden bingo ball. Every few moments we would hear another ball hit the gym floor around us.

There is no way of properly describing the feeling that overtakes you when something just appears out of nowhere and thrown at you by an unseen paranormal force. If that wasn't enough, we then heard one of the small balls bouncing in front of us! I could feel it's small vibrations on the floor. The sound was obviously just in front of me. I knew if I turned my flashlight on it I would see it bouncing. I didn't hesitate and clicked on my flashlight, and to my surprise, I could still hear it without seeing anything! So what's worse than having a wooden ball thrown at you from nowhere? The answer would be hearing one in front of you that isn't actually there at all.

I can still remember the drive home after the investigation had concluded. I was the passenger in the car with a friend of mine who had turned me on to the investigation. I remember us staring blankly and trying to process everything that had just happened to us.

My mind kept rushing back to "The Event" that Stacey and I endured in 1997. This investigation was that level of paradigm shifting activity. I went back once more with way too many people and too much gear, to be honest. The activity that second night included me almost fighting my best friend in the basement because we had each thought the other had touched them.

So, when Bonita from Pilgrim asked me if I may have another place with a great story that had never been on TV before…. I called back with the answer "I think I have your story."

John and the Ghost Brothers on set

The Ghost Brothers experience was awesome, as within five minutes of the start of our investigation I heard a disembodied voice. We had a boatload of evidence that night and truly focused on telling a story that had never been told to the world before.

You can watch that episode and judge it for yourself. All I can say is sometimes you don't have to visit a "World Famous Haunted Attraction" to experience a severe level of activity. The souls in the Cocke County War Memorial are angry, confused, and wanting someone to know their story. The question really is…what is that story? Hopefully someday we will all know and I also hope the light I shined on its dark history will lead us to the truth.

'Til Death & Beyond by John & Stacey Edwards

The Phantom Menace

The paranormal can be a terrifying field to be involved in, but it can also, at times, be rather humorous. Over the past two decades I have had many encounters on both ends of the spiritual spectrum.

The War Memorial was perhaps the most hardcore place I've ever been with a team. The things I experienced that night in 2004 still defy most any explanation I try to come up with. Everything from wooden bingo balls manifesting in the air and hitting me on the head, doors slamming so hard they got stuck, and several apparitions…all to be overshadowed by an EVP stating *"I was effin' Murdered!"* This place was as legit haunted as they get.

Even in the face of one of the most severe hauntings I had ever dealt with, I still found time to have a little bit of fun. Before I travelled to the location that night, I had stopped to eat at a Sonic Drive-In. In possibly not my wisest decision I've ever made, I downed two footlong chili cheese coneys and a Route 44 Dr Pepper before embarking into the mouth of Hell.

As the evening progressed, my stomach was already starting to rumble due to the stress and anxiety of the heavy activity occurring to me and the team. This night was a little odd as well because we were also working with another team out of nearby Knoxville, Tennessee. Basically a bunch of people I had never met before. That chili cheese demon was clawing his way out of my backside with some fierce power! In other words, I had some "phantom smells" randomly dropping all around me. The good thing was I was basically alone at this point and investigating an area where we had just heard a door slam.

As I was looking at the door in a hallway, I felt it may be as safe a time as any to relax my glutes and let my armed aroma fill the vacant hallway. Well, as fate has its ever special relationship with me, it was at this time a trio of young women decided to come help me investigate the slamming door.

I tell you there was no other choice at this point in time! I knew that, A.—I would never be working with these people again and B.—I would never lead anyone on again during an investigation—as I was just about ready to do. That's right! I had in one quick instant decided if they smelled it that I'm claiming Casper dealt it!

No way was I going to confess to three girls in their early twenties that I had just nearly ruptured my rear end by unleashing chili flakes all through this terribly haunted building! Needless to say, I was very much hoping that maybe it wasn't all that bad? Maybe it just floated on down the hall like a Doors song.

As it happened, the trio of talkative tarts reached the ground zero area, and let me just tell you, it was on like Donkey Kong! I heard my most feared whisper of the night as the biggest girl says "What is that smell? Oh my God! That's horrible! It smells like sulfur! Do you think?"…I was mortified. I had to think of my integrity in the field. Many thoughts went through my head at that moment, but not a single one of them was being honest about this particular colon cannon.

I looked at all three of them and said "oh, I don't really smell anything." Right about this time the worst possible thing that could have happened did. I felt it again and this time silence was in fact very much deadly. The timing was just too perfect as these girls were all sniffing like a Victorian-age blood hound after a rabbit.

The second one was so bad I was personally repulsed, and yeah, they got a full shot of round two. That was it! It is all kind of a blur after that moment. I just remember girls yelling out "DEMON" and running in all directions. I'm hoping the actual spirits that reside in that godforsaken War Memorial got as much of a kick out of that as I did.

The Phantom Menace

EVP's at a haunted theatre

Spirits of the Stage

I'm a firm believer that you can't give yourself a nickname. For those of you with self-afflicted nicknames, I absolutely am not intending to offend anyone…it's just one of those things I personally feel you have to earn from another's perspective of you. When I was a wrestler, I had a group of guys that performed as my followers and went by John Hawkins Promotions due to my stage name being John Hawkins. We also had a group of friends in the locker room who basically were my group of close friends. One of my closest friends referred to the group as J.H.P., and seemingly from that day on, so did all the fans. To this day many of the guys and fans from those days will actually refer to me as JHP as well. Sometimes things just happen in a very unexpected way. This happens to Stacey and I when it comes to investigating theaters.

It's not as if we have investigated every theater in the United States or anything. It's more of the connection we have always felt to these places and the incredible evidence we have collected along the way. There is something unnerving about standing on a stage in a pitch black theater while looking out at hundreds of empty seats. You can just feel the energy and emotions that have been expended on that stage.

Aside from performing as a professional wrestling talent for many years, I was also the lead singer of a hard rock band. I can tell you from a firsthand perspective that nothing in life compares to the feeling of having hundreds or even thousands of eyes focused entirely upon your performance.

You give everything you have inside, every ounce of passion, energy, and love into your character or music, comedy, or whatever you may be doing as an artist. There is something different about the artists of the world. Money isn't the motivation for any of the true artists I've encountered in my journeys. It's all about truly giving all you have and captivating the crowd, feeling the emotions pouring from them when you've successfully done your job.

I truly think these stages end up becoming paranormal flypaper for these emotional pipe bombs. If you believe a location can still be active because of some horrible tragedy years after it occurred, then why would a stage be any different? As I've said before, I have a hard time with the whole residual spirit thing, but I do believe in residual energy being layered on objects or even entire locations, the kind of energy that attracts spirits back to the site of some of their greatest moments in life.

One of the first theaters I investigated was the Barter Theater in Abingdon, Virginia. If you have never visited the historic town of Abingdon and want to experience a true feeling of supernatural energy, I highly encourage you to do so. There is history pouring from buildings such as The Martha Washington Inn, The Tavern, and the Barter Theatre.

There is also quite a substantial history to the subterranean cavern system beneath the town, as well as from the tunnels formerly connecting some of the buildings such as the Barter and the Martha Washington Inn. With stories of ghost horses, blood stains that will not go away, and an angry tunnel-dwelling spirit, how can you not love this place?

We investigated the Barter on two separate occasions and hopefully we will return a third time someday, as I feel there are still many questions left to answer. As for the Barter itself, the most reported spirit is of the founder, Robert Porterfield. He created the Barter Theater in 1933 and is sometimes seen sitting in the audience on opening night, or in the stage manager's booth. Actors consider a Porterfield spotting to be a sign of good luck, particularly before a show. Porterfield's spirit apparently likes to pull pranks on the stage crew.

The Barter Theater's rehearsal hall is haunted by the ghost of a housekeeper, who used to hold séances and imprison evil spirits in the theater's now locked Pyramid Room. She is supposedly heard yelling when people stay too late.

For us there were several incredible experiences inside the building. One was in the control room where we experienced physical manipulation of some objects. Another was the basement dressing rooms where the opening to the former tunnel lies. The tunnel is rumored to be home to an angry spirit who was murdered. The actors have reported being chased out of this area and up the stairs for many years. I can personally vouch for something being down there, as I kept an infrared camera pointing at the only exit on my first visit. You can watch the tape and see all of us leave and hear a voice clearly tell us to *"Get Out"* from right beside the camera.

The most unexplainable and heaviest of my experiences in the theater happened in a hallway. We were on our second visit to the building and had honestly not experienced as much as our first visit. We were wrapping up and collecting our cameras. Tim Clark (longtime team member) and I were with two hired camera people when out of nowhere we all experienced a feeling of vertigo followed by heavy bangs and an honest to God floor-shaking—all upon a very solid floor. It didn't last long, but it was one of those times when you could just feel the charged atmosphere.

Johnson City Community Theater

Our favorite theater was located in Johnson City, Tennessee and was called the Johnson City Community Theater (JCCT). The building was once a church, many years before they began running shows. We met some of our best friends in that location who were all connected to the operating of the JCCT. Frannie Miller (who is honestly the best human being on the planet), Kaeli and April Gardner, Rachel Helvey, and Joe Smith all helped us feel more than welcome that night and many nights thereafter. Frannie has been like a family member for

Stacey and I ever since.

The JCCT was absolutely active and really falls into the "energy left from the outpouring of love" category. The spirits were not evil, dark, or even mischievous. They would communicate with equipment, via EVP's, or by pulling Stacey's arm once. The ghostly inhabitants seem to be nothing other than former volunteers of the theater, except for one instance of a class A piece of audio recording of a man saying *"My Church You Got."*

We investigated this building more times than I can even remember and concluded it was indeed haunted. Our theater theory about returning performers or wandering spirits who felt that energy truly began with our investigations of the JCCT.

Other theaters with these feelings included one at a college, the State Theater in Kingsport, Tennessee, and the Kentucky State Theater in Lexington, Kentucky; where I learned a lesson about not acting tough when leading a public paranormal event at a haunted location! I can just say that building has a basement, that basement has a noisy ghost, and I left a recorder down there while Stacey had the rest of the group upstairs. I went to retrieve the recorder only to be greeted by some of the loudest knocks I've ever experienced! To the amusement of Stacey, I ended up being chased by the bangs all the way back up the steps! Yes—once. I ran once.

The funny thing is one of the most active locations we ever investigated on multiple occasions was a theater of a different variety. We were called in to investigate the Tri Cities Cinema 7 movie theaters in East Tennessee to see what was haunting the place.

There is plenty of mentions of things that occurred to us inside of this building scattered throughout this book. There was a boy named Billy, a poltergeist-type spirit that moves seats, and a truly dark force that helped spawn my Keeper theory.

The reason I mention it here is due to the emotions and energy given out in the theater, not directly from dedicated stage actors, but rather from delighted or even terrified moviegoers. The strange aspect to all of these cases is the large amount of evidence pointing to several spirits residing in each location. Could it simply be the large buildings? Could it be the fact they are empty most of the time? Or could it actually be connected to the power of emotional energy imprints?

We never set out to search for theaters to investigate. Over the years, however, it's seemingly become somewhat of a passionate part of our research. Likewise, I suspect a fisherman will more than likely return to the same spot he caught his largest number of fish. I feel a connection to the performance, we both feel the love of an artist, and we truly believe there is much to be learned from investigating theaters.

So step right up! Purchase your tickets now! The show is about to begin and everyone is just dying to perform for you.

'Til Death & Beyond by John & Stacey Edwards

The Black House

The twenty four foot Ryder truck was packed as tightly as humanly possible, and we were a broken family more than ready to move forward, to move away from the house in our side mirrors. We were in such a bad place at this point in time (early 2010) that we actually left many of our possessions inside the house.

We weren't exactly sure what caused all the strife in our little family then. What we did know was we had been through hell and back in the short span of four years living inside of this otherwise unassuming looking home.

Inside the truck cab there was me driving, Stacey riding shotgun, my little daughter Arianna, three years old at the time, and we were heading to our new apartment. Before we started to pull out, we asked Arianna if she was excited to move into our new place. Her adorable little face kind of scrunched up in that pondering type of way just before she said "I don't ever want to go back to The Black House."

The house was actually white and yes, she already knew the difference in colors. We didn't ask her anymore about the subject that day, as we all just knew. This house was indeed "Black," and something inside of the house or the land it was on had nearly done us all in. You sometimes hear people claim that "things were never the same," or "from that day on it all changed," and I can honestly tell you our good life truly began the moment we pulled away from "The Black House."

The house was built in the seventies, a split level, four bedroom family home, that had nothing special to it aside from being located in a very dark and ominous area. The things that happened to our family during our time in that house are almost too many to mention. We were under what we believe now to be, in hindsight, some form of a spiritual "oppression."

This "oppression" theory comes from the textbook symptoms we faced during our time there. We experienced strong emotional upheavals, financial problems, anxiety, acting out in ways that were simply not us, and that time period was the darkest, unluckiest, and hardest of our entire life, up to that point. It nearly tore our family completely apart, and in many ways our family was never completely the same again.

The Gap Creek area of Hampton, Tennessee where the Black House was located has a very dark history, dating all the way back to Native American stories of strange happenings occurring there. Any of your local books will talk about one or two stories originating from the area.

In the past few years, I had the chance to speak with Justin Guess of "The Haunt Masters Club" who told me he worked a case in that same area involving one of the only true demonic hauntings of his twenty years in the field. To say the least…it's a heavy and dark area of the world, and lies just on the edge of the Cherokee National Forest.

Stacey was working while I was staying home with our then one year old little girl. The house had been active with paranormal activity since day one. The only problem with saying that is, as we will later discuss, all of our homes in the early days of being together had recurring poltergeist-level activity. I don't think you ever "get adjusted" to such things happening, but you do what you have to in order to just keep living as normal as possible.

However, the type of activity occurring to us during this period was different than it had been anywhere else. It wasn't footsteps and doors slamming, but something rather intense in an entirely different manner. Several times I had been awakened after just falling asleep for a nap by a loud bang, always when alone with the baby. When I say "loud bang" I mean someone kicking the crap out of a door or a wall. I know this is a frequent paranormal claim many have had in the past, and often has somewhat of a natural explanation dealing with perception levels when trying to sleep—being different or heightened in near sleep or an almost lucid state versus being fully conscious and aware. Sort of like nodding off upright in a chair and jumping irrationally when you suddenly awake for fear of falling off the edge of the world. But this was indeed a very loud bang.

On this unfortunate morning I was super tired and Arianna was taking a nap on her blanket in the living room floor. I laid down to nap with her until she decided to wake up. Except it wasn't Arianna that woke me up. It was another voice entirely!

I found myself paralyzed except for being able to open my eyes. I was lying face down with my head turned facing the baby, and she was facing me. We were only about three feet away from one another. The voice I heard was your traditional horror movie demon voice. It was deep and terrifying, to be totally blunt about it.

The problem is, and always has been, with this, and a few other experiences…I can't even begin to tell you what it said! I just know I was being held down, paralyzed, and could only stare at my baby while being told something that seemed more like instructions than threats.

It lasted nearly two minutes, it seemed, and the entire time I was fighting to move my arms under me to raise up, but to no avail. After two minutes or so it was over. No sign of anyone. No repercussions or explanations. Just me sitting up in the living room floor of the black house with way more questions than answers…yet again.

Another time one of our older kids had a friend over for the weekend. She was taking a shower in our downstairs bathroom on a Saturday morning. The former owner's wife had passed away inside that bathroom. We never really felt or heard any evidence of this lady ourselves, as it always seemed to be the kids who experienced her presence in some way.

While this young teenage girl was taking her shower, she started screaming bloody murder. When she got out of the shower and told us what had happened, it took our breath away. She said she had seen a woman standing outside the shower—just staring at her. To say the least, I don't think she ever took a shower at our house again.

We had a pit bull named Starrdog Champion, after the Mother Love Bone classic song. Starr was one of our babies and would always sleep with Stacey. She was a sweetheart of a dog—until we moved into the house. After around six months, Starr seemed to completely lose her mind. She even tried attacking the kids and me! It was so sad for us because we love animals so much. We had to have her put down in one of the hardest things I've ever had to do in my lifetime. I even dug the hole and buried her in our backyard.

Around a year after moving in, I started despising this large angel statue that was in our front yard. The statue was actually beautiful and probably about four feet tall. One day I had all I could take and something possessed me to pull it down and drag it all the way to the woods behind our house. I pushed it over the hill to get it off of our property once and for all. To this day, I can't begin to tell you why I would have ever done anything like that. I only tell this part to better describe some of the weirdness associated with this house.

The kids all experienced things while living in the house, a black mass moving up and down the stairs, a woman walking across the downstairs and looking out of the window, doors that don't lock becoming locked and trapping them inside of rooms, and disembodied voices, amongst many other things.

We all exhibited behaviors that in no way shape or form resemble who we were or who we are. The house kept a heavy, oppressive, and deep feeling of hopelessness on all of us constantly.

The "People at the Door" was perhaps the epitome of weird happenings to occur during our time there, discussed in detail in the next chapter, but even after moving out the house continued to reach out to us with long, evil claws, as if not wanting to let us go.

After being compelled by my paranormal teammates to return and try to get answers, we eventually returned to the now vacant house to investigate it properly. The investigation yielded a full bodied apparition captured on Travis Moulden's handheld camcorder, EVP's so fierce and strong they are still replayed to this day, and the physical manipulation of a sealed window thrust open when seven witnesses just so happened to be staring in that direction.

After that last night, we never looked back again. I'm not sure what force it was that decided to get us out of the Black House, but I have a few guesses. We were locked up in a long mortgage, had no money to get out from underneath it, and were truly stuck in a place that was killing us until, at the seemingly darkest point, the unthinkable occurred.

The state of Tennessee decided to start a major highway project that would "just so happen" to go directly through our property. The state bought our house for the exact amount we needed to get away and start over.

In the following years we would hear various reports of the

destruction of the house, and the strange delays and problems the road crews had while trying to work in the area. It came as no surprise to us, and we made a pact we've kept for the past seven years—and counting—to never step foot in that county again.

Stronger together

For us, John and Stacey really began the day we found our path away from there. The healing and the hope started almost immediately, and within a year we were completely new people. It was like we were dating again; full of excitement, laughing, and exploring the unknown. It's hard to look back at some parts of our past, but none are more difficult than thinking back to the horror of the Black House.

THE BLACK HOUSE

'Til Death & Beyond by John & Stacey Edwards

The People
At The Door

It was a sunny and warm spring morning in Hampton, Tennessee. I was enjoying a little siesta with my baby daughter (a rarity) as the time of day was around 10AM. Although I was used to strange occurrences happening around me and to me, I could have never prepared myself for what I was about to experience on that otherwise normal weekday morning.

Sometimes, I would be awakened by loud knocking just as I was about to fall asleep, only to get out of bed and discover that nobody was knocking on any doors. During my time at the Black House, things like that had just become the unfortunate norm.

The neighborhood we lived in was a very quiet one with neighbors who never bothered with us and mostly older folks. When a car would make its way down my street, I would feel myself looking out the windows most of the time, because it was a rare occurrence to hear someone coming or going in the circle. This morning however, I never heard the car as I was sleeping, and I also didn't hear the knock before I heard the raucous laughter.

Something woke me up, and I can only make guesses as to who or what that might have been. Perhaps the woman who'd passed away in the downstairs bathroom and was occasionally glimpsed floating towards the windows by the kids was alerting me to danger, since Ari was also lying fast asleep.

Regardless of the "why," I woke up. The real story revolves entirely on what happened when I did. As I mentioned before, I heard laughing and cackling, but let me tell you this…it was freaking creepy, more of "A Clockwork Orange" kind of crazy vibe that I instantly felt occurring.

I'm six foot two of "never been scared of anything," and I found myself feeling severe anxiety simply from this diabolical laughter growing louder and louder. My worst fears were realized as the knocking began. It wasn't some run-of-the-mill "would you like to buy some thin mint cookies" kind of knocking either. This was "open up it's the po-po" variety of beating down a door.

In ten out of ten cases, I would march my big ass down the stairs, open up the front door, and smash someone's nose deep within their skull for beating on my door like they were attempting to wake the bleeding dead. This time I found myself absolutely terrified. Every hair on my body was standing on end and I was nearly paralyzed with an absolutely irrational fear.

A knock at the door always instills a certain sense of paranoia in the times we now live in. But I've never once before been so afraid to peek out of a window. I felt they would know I was peeking, would definitely be looking back up at me, and in this situation I felt like the intruder. In that moment I lost every ounce of "me" I had previously known.

As the beating on the door and laughing continued, I finally had all I could take, and my better sense of reality started sinking back in. So off to the window I went to check and see who was disturbing my sanity on this now very ominous and unusual Spring morning.

As I carefully crept over to the window to look down at my front porch, I could see the front door actually bending in from the force of the unnerving blows it was receiving. The thin lines of the outside daylight were sneaking inside from around the top right hand side of the door with every strike.

Ever so subtly, I used my index finger and my thumb to open a crease in the blinds to try and capture a glimpse of the unknown assailants. What I witnessed at that moment has haunted me more than almost anything I have ever seen, including the apparition of legs with no upper torso I spied at the Waverly Hills Sanatorium.

There were two people both beating wildly on my front door, one male and one female, both appearing to be young adults in their early to mid twenties. They were wearing clothes that appeared to come from a 1970's thrift shop, not only looking "out of time" but also unable to find something that fit properly; the attire not at all the correct size for either of these extremely thin and pale people.

My well-trained eyes quickly surveyed the immediate surroundings for some kind of vehicle, and I saw a nondescript clunker—not in my empty and very accessible driveway—but halfway into my front yard, already facing towards the road rather than the circle, as if ready for a quick getaway.

The girl had long brown hair and the guy had short "normal guy" hair. Nothing about the two of them would really stick out except for their weight and very pale complexion. Being a firm believer in the constitution of our great United States of America, I am a gun owner. Although I like to take care of things intelligently and without violence whenever possible, if you potentially threaten my safety or the safety of my family, then we will indeed have a serious problem.

I knew I needed to get my gun and open the door to confront this situation. I needed to get my faculties back in order and protect both my daughter and myself before they actually broke through the door.

Within the exact same moment of this Ted Nugent type thought hitting my primal 'Merica brain parts, the knocking ceased. The laughing was over and finished. Everything terrifying me was instantly gone. I turned to look back outside, but this time without trepidation. I wanted to see what in the actual hell was going on. I was mad, I was concerned, but most of all…I was no longer scared. When I fearlessly pulled open the blinds to see what 1970's Bonnie and Clyde were up to, they were gone…without a trace. I looked to see if I could get a plate number and call the cops, but the car had also vanished.

In a matter of maybe 15-20 seconds, the out of time couple, the Brady Bunch clothes, the pale and skinny bodies, and the Uncle Buck car were all gone.

To this day, I have no idea whatsoever how they could have even reached the car in that short amount of time, much less get in and leave without so much as a peep of a car door slamming, an old engine revving up or the peeling of rubber on my front lawn. This has been, and will continue to be, one of the oddest moments of my entire life.

'Til Death & Beyond   by   John & Stacey Edwards

Finding family history at the cemetery

The House of Edwards

Growing up a lot of kids have grandparents that live in a creepy house. Some even have grandparents that will tell them scary ghost stories just for fun. You know, the ones that help land you in therapy by age ten? Well, my paternal grandparents weren't those type of grandparents. They actually had so many freaking grandkids I'm not sure they actually realized which of us were at their house at any given time. But, the haunted house? Oh yes, they had a very haunted house! And the scary ghost stories? Well, go ahead and check that one off the list as well, except the stories were all real. Things that happened in that house were always weird.

The house was built sometime in the mid 1800's, a traditional farmhouse. It was built on and added to over the years, but the original parts of the house still remain. Unfortunately, both of my grandparents have passed on and the remaining family are relatively a bunch of crazy rednecks, so I don't have a reason to ever grace the doorstep again. What I do have is the memories and stories of many years of country fried hauntings.

The house is located in eastern Tennessee and sits on farm land. Legend has it that years ago the original lady of the house was cooking in the kitchen when her dress accidentally caught fire. She went up pretty quick, couldn't remove the clothes, and burned alive in the front yard of the house. Her ghost has been seen ever since in the house by many family members and visitors.

The Edwards side of my family isn't exactly the luckiest family in Tennessee. The number of untimely deaths are actually shocking, considering I have lost four first cousins that I played with in that house. Three of which were lost to very suspicious circumstances. Nearly every single family member has experienced high levels of weirdness during their life.

My dad is one who claims to have never experienced anything paranormal in the house, when in fact he has one of the craziest stories of the bunch. It's not a story about the house but it happened in the house. When he was a young boy, he had an issue with warts all over his hands and arms. The family knew a woman who could "heal" such afflictions. He said she gave him a wheat penny for each wart he had on him. The catch was he could never spend those wheat pennies or the warts would come back worse than ever. Dad took the wheat pennies and dropped them down one of those razor disposal slots in the medicine cabinet of the bathroom…I'll take witchcraft for $1000 Alex.

Speaking of witches…there was also a very colorful cast of characters over the years that came through the house. I remember the family talking about some of my Dad's brothers having relationships with women who performed witchcraft inside of the house.

When I first took Stacey for a visit, she was very creeped out. Stacey doesn't get creeped out at very much, unless there is good reason. She went to use the bathroom and we were all outside on the back porch, you always stay on the porch in the south. Next thing I know, Stacey comes outside all freaked out, asking me if I was screwing with her. After I assured her I wasn't and backed up by my Grandpaw, she told us that someone or something BANGED the absolute bejesus out of the bathroom door while she was washing her hands. She thought it was me messing with her, and quickly pulled the door open to scare me back—only to discover she was the only living person inside.

One night when my mom was still just the girlfriend visiting the house with my dad, she stayed overnight and slept downstairs. In the middle of the night, she had to use the bathroom, got up, and walked into the living room that leads to that bathroom. Once entering the living room she saw my grandmother standing with her back to her. My grandmother had a lot of Cherokee in her, and had this long black hair down to her ankles that she would let down when sleeping. It didn't take my mom very many times of saying "Mabel" without receiving an answer to figure out it wasn't my grandmother at all. As I said, that lady has been encountered numerous times in the history of the house.

When I was probably nine or ten years old, I remember staying the night and sleeping in one of the upstairs bedrooms. I slept on the floor with one of my cousins that night. We became incredibly creeped out with a feeling that something was up there with us. We actually heard it moving around in the hallway where moonlight just poured in at night. I covered my head with the blanket, as we all know will always shield you from danger, and my cousin bravely peeked out to actually see something supernatural in the hallway. I know he really saw something that night and it honestly creeps me out even writing this, because the only person I've ever shared that with is Stacey. I knew nobody would believe a couple of kids, because people never do.

My grandparents were married for well over half a century. One night, something went wrong and these two elderly people had a terrible and violent fight. The kids stepped in and made sure they were separated in different living quarters afterward. It was the saddest thing I've ever seen, as grandpaw never knew where my grandmother was. He would always ask us why he wasn't home and where she was. They both ended up dying while living estranged from one another, both never actually realizing it. A very sad ending that I only include because I don't believe in coincidences, and truly believe an evil force inside that house had something to do with it.

Stacey and I decided to investigate the house a few years ago. We received class A responses in every room that we tried to communicate. They were all of a male who said he knew my family, yet never would admit to actually being a part of my family. This story was one I debated on whether to include or not. I finally decided it belonged in the book because the weirdness of that house literally helped shape the haunted person I am today.

'Til Death & Beyond by John & Stacey Edwards

THE CONFEDERATE GHOST

This is a strange and beautiful world we occupy, filled with wild and wonderfully unexplainable events. Some of us choose to explore these events or phenomena with an open mind to discover and uncover life's ever-growing mysteries. The funny thing is, when you start looking around every corner or underneath every stone, the amount of the unexplainable seems to multiply like rabbits. There have been many events throughout my years that are unexplainable in one sense, but in another way, seem to make all the sense in the world. I want to share one of these events with you.

As I've previously stated, my mother became ill more than a decade ago with the horrible disease known as Lupus. She has always been one of the more brutally honest human beings I have ever known, and probably where I get some of that. She has a very solid Christian belief, that at times makes it rather difficult to accept my pursuit of answering paranormal questions. I personally believe her strong opinions of what I do stem more from the fact she herself has dealt with so much unexplained phenomena in her life. We shared a very bizarre event early in my life that she was never able to fully explain away.

The Lupus attacks her body and has caused many other ailments that have left her confined to her bed most all day, every day. She is on heavy medication and thus people may take a story of a ghostly visit with a grain of salt. I, however, am not "people"…I am her son and know my mother well enough to know she experienced something.

Mom said she was in bed and was being held down by a tall man in a confederate uniform. He introduced himself as Hezekiah, and told her how much he despised the Edwards side of my family, something I can understand and totally agree with at times—insert heavy sarcastic tone here. It was a very strong story to swallow, even with the sheer clarity of the event. Mom wasn't the only person to experience strange phenomena in this same bedroom, though. My aunt was over for a visit one day, walked down the hallway, and shrieked in terror, according to my parents. What she went on to describe was seeing the apparition of a man. Stacey and I stayed at the house for around a month in late 1999, and Stacey also experienced heavy, strange feelings in the same room.

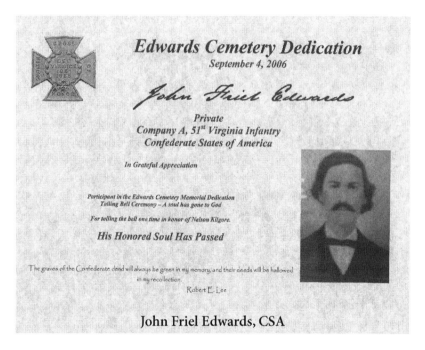

My father was engaged in the pursuit of his genealogy a few years back. In his research he found many interesting ties to the past. Among these discoveries were ties to royalty, family origins in Wales, heroes, criminals, and some ancestors we already knew of, such as the Confederate soldiers. My great great Grandfather, John Friel Edwards, served in the 51st Virginia infantry until being captured and imprisoned in Fort Delaware. The ties with John Friel never seem to let up. He became a major piece of my Major Graham Mansion investigation, and needless to say, is named John Edwards like my father and I.

One warm September afternoon in 2006, my father asked me along for a Confederate dedication ceremony in Virginia at a graveyard that bears my family name. I have never been very into genealogy or

The Confederate Ghost

into any sort of reenactments of days gone by. My opinion has changed since that day when I saw the passion expressed by these descendants of the soldiers. The organizers of the event greeted me with the normal pleasantries as my father and my late grandfather proudly paraded me around to the other attendees of the event.

I noticed rather quickly that I was amongst the youngest of the spectators, and I was perhaps witnessing a dying art. I didn't expect to feel such an overpowering rush of honor overtake me before arriving. This short, blonde lady explained all of the day's events to us and the order of things. A certain group of descendants were supposed to have their name called after a speech to receive a flag and a certificate of commemoration for their honorable ancestor and veteran of the 51st Virginia infantry in the Confederate army. Dad was informed he was going to accept for John Friel Edwards, my aforementioned great great Grandfather, and I was going to stand by taking pictures.

As the proceedings were about to commence, I was informed of a slight problem. There was one man who had no descendants present at the ceremony. After hearing of this injustice, I quickly stood up and told the blonde lady I would be honored to accept the certificate in order to honor the memory of this fallen soldier. She was very excited about my decision, and to be direct, it's really out of my character to do something like this, but I felt compelled by something larger than I fully understood.

After the ceremony was over and everything went off without a hitch, we drove around this backwoods area of Virginia where my late grandfather grew up. I cherish that day now more than ever, since losing my grandfather to old age not long after. He was so excited to point out streams he had once played in, or meadows he had once ridden horses in. That September day is now etched in my mind, if not for the paranormal implications as much as the fact it was the last time I truly "hung out" with Grandpaw.

When my father and I once again reached his house, I was worn out and decided to go inside for a bit before driving all the way back home. When we walked inside, Dad was excited to tell Mom about the day's events and how they unfolded. He was particularly interested in telling her about receiving the flag and the certificate. As my mother sat in her prescription chair examining the certificate of John Friel Edwards, she, being the keen eyed detective she is, asked what certificate and flag I was holding. Dad then began to explain what I had decided to do in honor of a man nobody had showed up to honor.

My mother asked me if she could see the certificate, as if she already knew something was going to be of the odd flavor. Upon glancing at the certificate, my mother brought her hand up to her mouth and clasped it tightly as if to hold back a frightened gasp. "Do you even know who this is John?!" my mother frantically exclaimed.

"No clue, Mama," I halfheartedly replied, trying to not pour gasoline on what appeared to be the start of an obvious three alarm fire. She then looked at my father and I saw his eyes open as wide as the first time I had seen breasts on a scrambled Cinemax movie as a child.

Mom looked me in the eyes and said, "It's him, it's the man from my room, it's Hezekiah!" I looked down at the paper to read the name, already well aware of what I was going to see. The name on the certificate was indeed the name my mother identified as the Confederate soldier visiting her at night that hated my family.

I believe firmly that there are things in this world we are not meant to fully understand. My mom knew right at that moment that what her son had unintentionally done was honor the memory of a man who would have otherwise been dishonored. An Edwards had gone out of his way to help Hezekiah that day. My mother, to this day, has had no more visits from the angry Confederate soldier. As I previously stated, there have been many events throughout my years that are unexplainable in one sense, but in another way make all the sense in the world. This was truly one of those occasions that just so happened to occur deep within the Haunted South.

THE CONFEDERATE GHOST

'Til Death & Beyond by John & Stacey Edwards

The Curious Case of Mary Bateman

Spirits are often unclear and cryptic when they give messages from the other side. Often, when John gets a message, it comes in bits of seemingly random words and phrases. Being a puzzle lover, I immediately take the pieces of information and try to figure out what they mean, who the message is for, and why John was given the information. This can be both satisfying and frustrating at the same time, such as in the curious case of Mary Bateman.

In early 2013, John received a message from the spirit of a woman. This was still in the early stages of having his gift, so he often couldn't block spirits, especially strong spirits, from just popping in and communicating whenever they wanted. This spirit was insistent.

"They're looking at me. I don't like it. Make them stop."

That was her message. The only other information she gave was her name: Mary Bateman.

This wasn't a lot of information to go on, and I was sure this would be one of the times I would end up frustrated. I mean, it didn't make any sense. Who could be looking at her? Who could even see her? Still, I did some research to see what I could find, and I was blown away by what surfaced.

Mary Bateman, also known as the "Yorkshire Witch," was born in 1768. She was well known in Leeds as a fortune teller and for having the ability to make potions to ward off evil spirits. In 1809, Mary was arrested for fraud and murder. Although she claimed to be innocent, the court found her guilty and she was hanged on March 20, 1809 for the murder of Rebecca Perigo. After her execution, her body was put on public display. Mary's body was one of the first to be publicly dissected in the quest for medical knowledge.

During the course of my research, I found out her remains were on display at the Thackray Medical Museum in Leeds. People were looking at her!

The message seemed pretty clear, but I wasn't sure what to do about it. How was I going to contact a museum in England and tell them the spirit of a woman, whose skeleton was currently on display, wanted me to let them know that she was unhappy about being looked at, and could they please take her down? I did email the museum and inquire about the display in hopes of finding a way to bring up the subject. The museum did not respond, however, and I eventually just let it go and didn't think about it again.

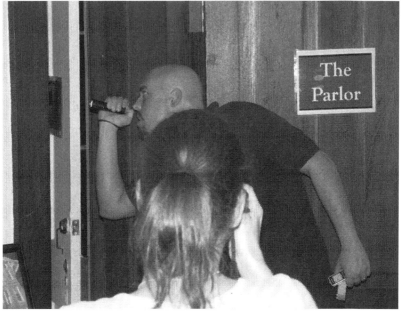

Searching for spirits

At the end of that year, John got a message that was just a date, January 14th. The date was important, but we had no idea why. When January 14th arrived, we were eager to see what was going to happen, but it seemed like just an ordinary day. John came home from work and we were sitting in the bedroom trying to figure out what was special about the date.

While we were talking, John saw a light float into our bookcase and into a book. I could not see the contents of the bookcase from where I was sitting, but I could see the look on John's face. He told me what he saw, and I immediately went to the bookcase and peered at the shelves. He couldn't read the titles from where he was sitting, but he directed me to a smaller book with a green cover where the light had landed. The book was called *"A Ghost A Day."* In the book is a different ghost story for every day of the year. We took this as a sign and opened the book to the story for January 14th. The story listed for that day was for a haunted building in Yorkshire, England. It was a sign. A message to remind us of what we forgot, the Yorkshire Witch, Mary Bateman.

So I once again made an effort to help her. Instead of being coy and vague, I just sent a message to the museum with the whole story. I explained about Mary and how upset she was about the display. Again, I didn't hear anything back, but I wasn't expecting to. I'm sure they thought I was a lunatic, but I delivered the message anyway.

Mary never visited us again after that. I emailed the museum again recently, just to ask if they still had the display. I received a nice reply informing me that the display had been taken down in 2015 and sent back to Leeds University.

'TIL DEATH & BEYOND BY JOHN & STACEY EDWARDS

The Truck Stop

For some it's the famous James Dean Porsche dubbed "Little Bastard" that not only killed James Dean, but has been rumored to have been linked to several other injuries or deaths in the years since Dean's death. For others, it's "The Curse Of The Bambino," or even "The Madden Curse," that your mind first jumps to when the subject comes up.

Unfortunately, there are many lesser known and much darker curses out there. I believe a curse is a strange force due to the fact it normally seems to take a belief in the curse to make it really work. This is obviously not always the case, but I have seen curses actually work firsthand.

There is a special little curse book we own that Stacey keeps well hidden from me. The reason is I may or may not have tried one that actually worked! Not because I'm a dark wizard, but because I'm too curious for my own good sometimes. I would never attempt anything like that these days, as I know all too well the power of words, thoughts, and intent.

In this particular case, the other party had no idea of the curse, and it still seemed to work. Most of the time though, our minds have a power all their own that I feel can create a positive or negative action to occur, simply from the faith and belief we invest in the idea of the curse, spell, prayer—or anything of that variety.

One of the strangest things that has ever happened to me regarding a supposed "curse" occurred in 2008. The world of professional wrestling is filled with a strange breed of characters. Wrestling, in this form, derived from the carnival circuits of the 19th century. We even spoke a form of "carny" in the ring and in front of fans to keep what we were discussing secret.

Pro Wrestling is a brotherhood like no other. We would literally put our lives in each other's hands night after night, bleed buckets of blood, and take incredibly long road trips packed together in a car for little to no monetary gain. For the ones who do it...it's hard to describe to someone on the outside. Many of those old carnival superstitions seemingly carried over into the wrestling business.

I can recall countless stories of haunted locker rooms, crazy UFO sightings during trips on remote backroads, and several superstitions we would all follow, due to what happened "to ol' so and so one time when he didn't adhere to taking the correct route to a town," or perhaps didn't enter through the correct door when entering the arena.

One of these superstitions had to do with our road trips to wrestle in West Virginia, where a bunch of us would work quite often. My guys and I were heels, the bad guys, on West Virginia TV, and pretty notorious. It was always a lot of fun, but I always kept a real job that was normally in retail management. This "shoot job," shoot meaning real, would normally mean I was always in a hurry to make it back home as quickly as possible after one of our shows.

A rough night wrestling as a "heel"

The Truck Stop

We would always set off from Kingsport, Tennessee and travel up to Wytheville, Virginia, and then on up to our West Virginia destinations. The story was that there was a well known curse for the trips home. On your trip back to Tennessee, you absolutely had to stop at this particular truck stop in Wytheville, Virginia, or else.

What would happen if you didn't stop at said truck stop? Well, it varied depending on who you were talking to. Since I was already involved in the paranormal field, it deeply interested me as to why this story began, who figured it out, and what exactly happened if you ignored the provisions of the curse.

For dozens of these trips, I never once disobeyed the preexisting rules of the road. As time wore on I really doubted the legitimacy of the supposed curse, and even made fun of it—but still stopped at the truck stop every single time. I enjoyed the stop to use the bathroom, get snacks, and play this stupid coin game.

One night however, we were severely late getting out of West Virginia. It was well past 2AM by the time we even hit Virginia, and I had to work the next morning. There was no way I was going to be able to stop. My decision was perfectly fine with three of the passengers riding with me in the van. Another wrestler riding shotgun, Beau James, wasn't interested whatsoever in tempting fate. Beau loudly voiced his displeasure at my decision, but alas, he wasn't the one driving. As we passed by the exit for the truck stop, the argument seemed to quiet down and we progressed to talking about how crappy someone else's match had been on the card that night. I think a good twenty miles had passed and we were engulfed in a completely new conversation with no thought whatsoever about the curse…

Out of nowhere there was a full size truck tire in the middle of the road. We were going about 85MPH and the tire was laying flat—but it was tire, wheel, and everything. There was no missing it as we didn't see it until the very last moment.

I'll never forget the van lifting off of the ground, the way time seemingly stopped, the screams coming from a van full of giant men, and the unbelievable amount of sparks all around us when we hit the pavement again. I'll never be able to explain just how I kept the van under control as we came crashing back down.

As I kept driving, everything was absolutely silent. Not a single word from any of the passengers or me. We all were trying to let our minds process what just happened and how lucky we were to still be alive, when all of a sudden there was a voice breaking the silence beside me.

"I told you that you should have stopped…" I never failed to stop at that damn truck stop ever again.

THE TRUCK STOP

'Til Death & Beyond by John & Stacey Edwards

Where's the Other Guy?

In the Summer of 2008, I remember being super excited to once again be investigating the Waverly Hills Sanatorium in Louisville, Kentucky, one of my all time favorite locations. I was with Tim, Connie, and Ashleigh Clark who were, and will always be, just like family to us.

This particular evening, we were getting our gear ready to go inside the ominous structure for our overnight investigation when Tina Matherly, the co-owner of Waverly, drove up on her golf cart.

Tina says, "Hey, I want to leave this up to you guys, but this guy wants to join you all tonight."

"Who on Earth wants to join us?" I asked.

"Um, I can't remember his name. He played Jason Vorhees in Friday the 13th."

"Kane freaking Hodder?!" I exclaimed with serious excitement, as I am actually a huge fan of all horror movies.

I can't remember if it was only one or two seconds before I said yes. Regardless, there I was, locked inside the most haunted building in the United States with Jason Vorhees! Pretty insane to say the least. Tina let us know that he really wanted to see the place and experience something.

Now, Kane has committed more murders on screen than any other actor in cinematic history and has "KILL" tattooed inside his bottom lip. I'm a big dude and he still has a good inch on me in height. He's a super cool dude though, and I wanted him to have a great experience.

The night was not a letdown, Waverly never is, with activity in all forms. The problem was Kane wasn't really experiencing anything.

Sometimes when you have a guest with you on an investigation, there comes this moment where you seemingly can't get anything to happen, because you simply want to have it happen so bad. It's a very strange and very frustrating feeling. It reminds me of having a terrible pain—right until the moment you finally get to see the doctor.

We were on the first floor investigating with Kane, a random lady, and my compadre, Tim Clark, who had been on dozens of investigations with me by this point. We sat in the first room for maybe half an hour asking questions during a "call and response" EVP session with very little happening. I did however hear something moving to my left during different times of the session.

The way we were set up, Kane was on one end of the room beside the lady, Tim across the room from me filming, and I was alone on my side of the room nearest the door.

After finishing the session, we decided to walk to the very next pharmacy room on the first floor for another session. This is when everything became very interesting, and honestly rather freaky for me and Tim.

While we were all standing in the pitch dark room, we were talking with our flashlights turned on, and all of a sudden Kane says, "Where's the other guy?"

"What other guy, dude?" I said.

"Come on man don't try fuckin' with me, the guy that was sitting right beside you!"

"Um, Kane, dude, it was just me…only me…on that side of the room."

At this point, the tension in the room could have been cut with a knife. Kane was obviously running all of this through his mind and I was very glad I had not participated in any sex recently, just in case the Jason within him came out to attack me…it felt very much like that could happen at any moment.

I was a pro wrestler and held a job that required me to fight criminals on a daily basis, but this was the king of all murderers and an accomplished Hollywood stuntman. I'm not sure how that fight ends up, but it's one of those times you find yourself happy that cooler heads prevailed.

The absolute coolest thing I know is, and Tim knows, that Kane Hodder finally experienced something paranormal, and didn't even realize it. We still talk about that crazy night to this very day.

Paranormal Sideshow fan art by Allen Marston

WE ARE ALL STRANGE HERE

Within the pages, stories, theories, and ramblings of this book, we have explored many strange and unexplained occurrences that have deeply influenced the course of our life. John and Stacey wouldn't be John and Stacey without the good, the bad, the ghosts, the demons, the aliens, and mostly—the weirdos we befriended along the way.

While we don't agree with every opinion out there, we take pride in the fact that we respect each and every opinion we hear. We feel you need to always keep an open mind when listening to someone telling you about their cat using his mind control to influence their dog into peeing on the bed. Who are any of us to truly say it's not happening? Have you spoken to a cat using your telepathy lately?

The more strange phenomena we study, the more we find to add validity to it. The worst thing any of us can do is dismiss things without actually investigating it for ourselves.

There was a time I personally rejected anything from supposed psychics. I knew strange intuition came to me often. I knew sometimes I would dream of things that would eventually come to pass. I knew my mother and my grandmother both would know when I was somewhere I shouldn't be, and actually found me there every time.

Even though I was armed with this knowledge, I still wanted no part of it to be included in my research or on my paranormal teams. As discussed in the "How Did You Not Hear That?" chapter, that view changed dramatically when my gifts went from odd coincidences to unbelievable and accurate occurrences.

I have dreamt of a particular date that was nearly two years in the future, only to see that day arrive and be the date of a close family member giving birth to their first child. I also woke from a particularly lucid dream that had me walking through the grounds of a compound.

I described it all in great detail including the fact I had seen two shetland ponies. Years later, Stacey and I started recording our podcast at a strange compound (for lack of a better description) that matched the dream. The crazy part was when I was describing this dream to the owner of the studio, he looked shocked and surprised at the same time. He then went on to tell me that just behind his house there were two Shetland ponies out of the sight from everyone.

The only reason I share this is because it better serves to explain the fact we just don't know everything. Whether you're a Ghost, UFO, or Bigfoot hunter, you need to cooperate and respect everyone who is honestly in pursuit of the unknown.

There was once a time that the hunt for paranormal programming was almost as hard as searching for a photogenic Sasquatch. Truth be told, up until the late nineties, and more so, the early two thousands, there were only a handful of programs available. One reason for this could be that there were way fewer channels available. I think a bigger reason is that almost every human being now has some sort of camera or camcorder with them at all times.

The early shows were freaking scary! The topics had never before been explored without someone being burned at the stake, or in the very least, being cast out of the village. Ok, that may be a little bit of an exaggeration, but in all actuality, when someone spoke about demons, aliens, Bigfoot, or even a Lady in White, they were always met with a healthy dose of skepticism and ridicule from society.

One of those early shows that still resonates inside of my hammer horror loving mind is a tasty little gem known as "In Search Of." This show was the absolute greatest show ever created to scare the crap out of everyone. It sparked so much imagination in my five year old mind and caused so many people to start telling their own stories or explore their own adventures into the unknown.

It was hosted by a Vulcan and had real footage of real creatures and strange mysteries. Ok, so maybe he wasn't really a Vulcan, but they really did have the aforementioned creature footage. Honestly, I can only remember watching one episode even though I know I watched it religiously with my Dad.

The episode etched in my memories revealed the infamous "Patterson Footage" into my impressionable preteen mind. The

Patterson-Gimlin Film is footage purportedly captured on the afternoon of October 20, 1967 in a California forest. By the time I witnessed the film, it had already been the subject of countless talk shows and documentaries.

The validity of the footage is of little concern to me these days. The undeniable mark it left on me is the most important thing for this discussion. You see, I am reasonably certain we have yet to discover all of the mysteries on our planet, in our oceans, and underneath our crust. It seems plausible to me that considering the fact we had no clue about the existence of mountain gorillas until 1902 that Bigfoot more than likely does exist.

The paranormal television shows are extremely important to the continuation of research into the strange, bizarre, and unknown mysteries of our world. In my opinion, we live in a society that has lost touch with its roots of adventure and thirst for knowledge. Most people seem way more interested in the newest trending video on YouTube than solving the riddle of Stonehenge.

For me, the claim that thousands of our fellow humans have been abducted by aliens should be the top concern of some government hearings or research. A haunting that results in deep scratches or physical manipulation should have some major funding by a college to figure out why. A family of eight foot tall missing links should, in the very least, be searched for with the full cooperation of the scientific community. But, we all know, this almost never happens.

Although I am sure science is never wrong: the Earth is flat, we are the center of the universe, and the Earth is 4000 years old, just for starters, it can from time to time need to be challenged. And as long as the mainstream elite are more concerned with covering up the truth and controlling their sheep, than with education and searching for the answers of the world's greatest riddles, it will take the likes of you, me, and every forward thinking soul to explore on our own.

Mysterious booms have been one of my top clicks over the last seven years. The true mystery to these events for me is the fact that mainstream media completely ignores it. If Kim Kardashian wears a dress that doesn't correctly match her shoes it becomes an international incident. But, when sky trumpets blow in every country on the planet with absolutely zero explanation given to us from the scientific community…it really bothers me.

If you stop reading this book right now and search "Mysterious Booms" on YouTube, you will find literally hundreds of videos from local news stations reporting on loud booms happening in communities or cities across the world. This is primarily a phenomenon I see happening in the continental United States, but it has been widely reported internationally as well.

Sometimes these "Booms" may sound like a cannon firing and be accompanied by shaking like a small tremor. The problem is that many times it rarely shows up as a measurable event, which leaves homeowners with cracked walls frustrated and concerned.

The "Sky Quakes" are lumped in with the mystery booms, but, for me at least, they seem like something different. They sound like we are hearing the bleed from another dimension trying to rip and claw its way into our own.

This is definitely a rabbit hole as deep as "The Mandela Effect," just listen to our podcast to fall into that little gem, and I don't see us climbing out of it anytime soon.

Something has shifted folks. Something is just different than it was before. When I was a kid, I never remember weekly reports of large fireballs streaking over seven states—including Kentucky, because somehow it can happen in Bangladesh yet Kentucky will still claim to have also witnessed it. I never remember sink holes on a weekly basis, Mysterious Booms, Sky Quakes, Mandela Effects, or many of the high-strangeness that seems to be a very common occurrence these days.

The mainstream theories explaining these things are in abundance and all pretty ridiculous, because many times they may explain one occurrence, but not all. Or like a great television paranormal debunker would say, "if a car drives on its back two wheels at a speed of 19 and a half mph on a full moon in mid October…it could possibly cast a shadow onto this window that would scare the window into making a footstep noise."

Stacey and I just so happen to have been affected by both the paranormal and ufology personally. Because of this little truth nugget, we realize how similar the fields actually seem to be. Will the UFO gang ever hang out with the Ghost Hunting guys? Will either of them ever take the Cryptozoology gang seriously? I can't answer that question because, for us, we are all strange here.

The truth is we don't know what the truth is, and sincerely need to keep an open mind to all strange phenomena. It could all be connected (I'm looking at you CERN), or it could just be a shift in our reality due to everyone starting to wake up. All I know is we will keep looking and listening with our eyes, ears, and minds wide open. So, for my lovely wife, Stacey, my name is John Edwards, and we both intend on continuing our pursuit of the unexplained Til' Death do us part…or maybe, just maybe, even after.

Taking a break at Fort Knox

About the Authors

John and Stacey Edwards started their journey into mystery way back in 1997 when they shared a paradigm shifting paranormal experience together. The "Event" sent them down a road not too many other people were traveling back in 1997…investigating the paranormal.

In the two decades since deciding to follow this path together, they have produced many documentaries, investigated hundreds of locations, and hosted several Paranormal Podcasts.

They have also successfully managed a family that has produced several little goblins as well. John and Stacey recently celebrated their twentieth wedding anniversary. Their love has only grown stronger each and every year…a bond strengthened in the trials of the haunted lives they live.

From being involved in Professional Wrestling, fronting a local heavy metal band, being featured on the Ghost Brothers television show, to being an executive for a fortune 300 company, you seriously are in for a ride with this couple!

John and Stacey can be heard weekly hosting The Paranormal Sideshow Podcast available via iTunes, Googleplay, Spotify, iHeartRadio, or wherever and however you like to listen to your podcasts!

Facebook: Facebook.com/ParanormalSideshow

Twitter: @sideshow97

On instagram @johnandstaceyedwards

YouTube: YouTube.com/paranormalsideshow

On patreon: Patreon.com/paranormalsideshow

Made in the USA
Columbia, SC
04 September 2019